WHY WOMEN FAIL

WHY WOMEN FAIL

Achievement and Choice for Modern Women

ANN DALLY

WILDWOOD HOUSE LONDON
BOOKWISE AUSTRALIA

First published in Great Britain 1979

Wildwood House Limited
1 Prince of Wales Passage
117 Hampstead Road
London NW1 3EE

In Australia by Bookwise Australia Pty Ltd,
104 Sussex Street, Sydney, 2000.

Copyright © 1979 Ann Dally

ISBN 0 7045 3010 4

Typeset by Inforum Ltd, Portsmouth
Printed and bound in Great Britain by
Redwood Burn Ltd, Trowbridge and Esher

W11799 /5.95 . 2.80

Contents

For
Emma, Jane, Mandy, Prudie and Zoë

Introduction

Something dreadful is happening to women. Not directly to all women but to a sufficient number to affect nearly all women and indeed society as a whole.

This dreadful thing – for it is to be dreaded – is self-destructiveness, that strange process by which humans sometimes damage or destroy themselves in body, mind or spirit.

Self-destructiveness has always been with us and it is not confined to women. One might expect that the great advances that women have made in recent years, the improvements in their position and the increasing opportunities open to them would decrease the amount of self-destructiveness among them. But this is not the case. In spite of these advances and, in my contention, because of them, self-destructivness is increasing among them. Although many women are flourishing with choice and opportunities which would never have been theirs in former times, more and more women are being driven into self-destructiveness or are being encouraged by various means to bring out their latent self-destructive tendencies.

In an age when women have achieved so much, why are so many in conflict with themselves and with those they most care about? Women can now find fulfilment in many ways that would have been impossible even a generation ago, so why is self-destructiveness so widespread and apparently increasing among them? Why, for instance, is there an epidemic, chiefly among women, of drug over-dose, wrist slashing and other self-destructive acts now labelled collectively 'suicidal gesture' (which used to be called 'attempted suicide'), so that this has become the commonest cause of emergency admission to hospital? Why have the last twenty years seen an epidemic of self-starvation in young women, often requiring treatment by psychiatrists and admission to psychiatric hospitals? Why is there so much child-battering, mostly by women? Why are so many depressed? Why do so many suffer from agoraphobia and fear to leave their homes, even to go shopping? Why do far more women than men visit doctors, especially for symptoms without physical cause and why is this number increasing? Why do so many more women than men take sedatives, sleeping pills, tranquillizers and anti-depressant drugs? Why are alcoholism and violence, both traditionally men's problems, increasing in women? Why do more women than men attend psychiatrists and why are more admitted to mental hospitals? Why do so many more women than men suffer from overt anxiety and psychosomatic complaints? Why do so many women feel empty or lacking in motivation? In an age of choice, why do so many feel that they have no choice? Why do so many women have such low self-esteem? Why are attempts to alleviate this state of affairs so seldom successful?

Further questions arise from these. What have women actually achieved in our time? They now have new opportunities, but what exactly are these opportunities and what is the price that has to be paid? Is the apparent improvement in the position of women a sham that actually leads to suffering? Do the changes in their position benefit the majority of women but overwhelm a minority? Are some women simply unable to cope with them? Why do so many women dislike the women's movement and speak contemptuously of 'women's lib'? Why do these include many who themselves dislike the traditional rôle and who take advantage of the new freedom for women? Why is it that even women who believe strongly in equal opportunities and in the sharing of rôles, and who benefit greatly from the new awareness that has come through the women's movement, still express hostility and perpetuate its early aggressive image? What has the women's movement actually achieved and why do we have it at all? What, if any, is the connection between achievement and self-destructiveness? And lastly, what might be done to improve the situation?

This book has been written in my spare time from practice as a psychiatrist. I see many self-destructive men but many more self-destructive women. I have come to know many of them intimately and I have also met many in other spheres of my life so I know that they are not all psychiatric patients. One question is often in my mind. What is this self-destructiveness all about? The book aims to explore these questions from the point of view of both the individual and of society, and I shall try to make positive suggestions for society in general, and women in particular. I hope it will help to prevent self-destructiveness in women from becoming even more widespread than it already is, crushing and undermining what has been achieved and is still to be achieved.

Self-destructiveness takes many forms. In a previous book *The Morbid Streak: Destructive Aspects of the Personality* I discussed the ways in which we destroy ourselves and others and examined not only the most obvious forms of destructiveness such as suicide and murder but also destructive personality traits, neurosis and despair, perversion and martyrdom. I included such things as boredom, superficiality, lack of imagination and self-deception. I explored the areas of feeling and behaviour that are associated with frustration, pain and anxiety and their connection with destructiveness. I tried to show that certain characteristics and aspects of human behaviour are better understood if they are regarded metaphorically as annihilation of parts of the self, allied to suicide and more obvious forms of destructiveness. This exploration led to a study of imagination and imaginative processes and their bearing on some of the troubles of our time. I concluded that we need to allow free rein to imaginative capability in order best to survive the special problems faced by western civilization today.

In this book I shall develop those ideas and examine them from a less theoretical and more practical point of view, contrasting them with achievement and applying them particularly to women in our own time. One of my aims is to look at achievement and self-destructiveness and the ways in which they affect individual women and their families and also women in general, and, through them, society. I do not believe that, in this age of opportunity for women, the extent of their self-destructiveness is fully realized because much of it is hidden or disguised. I believe that greater understanding of it will not only help many people but will also help to improve the position of women and thus, indirectly, that of their husbands, children and associates.

Chapter One

Women in Conflict

The epidemic of self-destructiveness among women in the western world is probably the result of recent changes in our society and may be just a phase through which we have to pass. But self-destructiveness has become so widespread and so damaging that it could wreck much of the progress that has been made or cause much delay to it. I also believe that at present we are doing little to prevent it because we have as yet not fully identified or classified the situation and the problems. Only by doing this can we move towards a solution.

Self-destructiveness is thought, fantasy or action that prevents or destroys development or fulfilment of personal life. It may be active, as it is in its extreme forms: suicide, suicidal gesture, self-poisoning, both quick and slow with drugs or alcohol, or in the pursuit of some aim or relationship that will have self-destructive consequences. It may be passive, as when people allow themselves to be damaged or destroyed in mind or body or when they fail to care for themselves or to take necessary steps for their development or fulfilment. It can be physical or emotional, solitary or social, and it is often best understood in a family setting.

Self-destructiveness reflects inability either to cope with the problems of living or to find satisfaction in life. It underlies many of the problems both of individual women and of the women's movement and is one of the biggest handicaps that women face today. It reveals an inability to choose constructively in a world of choice or to find a positive way out of dilemmas created by choice. It often shows as an unwillingness or inability to become involved in anything at all, or in anything outside such narrow fields as cleaning a house or planning a wardrobe. Even time-honoured female preoccupations such as devoting oneself totally to finding and catching a man or to pleasing one who has been found and caught, are liable, in our society, to be self-destructive. Society is still full of messages to women encouraging them to behave in this way, for example in advertisements, but in fact no longer supports them if they do. This tends to create vicious circles and conflict. The result is often some form of self-destructiveness.

Self-destructiveness does not, of course, exist in all women but is so widespread among them that we are all, both men and women, affected by it. The self-destructiveness of thousands of others affects you and me and any self-destructiveness in us affects others. At present, when the position of women in our society is improving, many women are undeveloped and unfulfilled more because of their own or others' self-destructiveness than from lack of opportunity. This is a reversal from the days when they were hampered mainly because of lack of equality and opportunity. This self-destructiveness is frequently responsible for slow progress in the advance of women and for failure to take advantage of acknowledged opportunities. Self-destructiveness in women is probably now more important than male chauvinism in hampering the development of women and the women's movement. So where does all this self-destructiveness come from?

I am not implying that self-destructiveness is virtually confined to women, or that it is basic to woman's personality or biological function. Most of the types of self-destructiveness described in this book are also found in men and some are commoner among men than among women. These include suicide, (the ultimate self-destructive act), and also alcoholism and the relentless pursuit of financial or professional disaster. The self-destructiveness of men affects women too and may or may not interact with their own self-destructiveness. But I believe that most types of self-destructiveness are commoner in women than in men because, for reasons that will be discussed in this book, women are more vulnerable. This vulnerability comes not from any direct inherent or biological weakness but from the difficult and changing position of women at the present time and from the conflicts this sets up which lead to self-destructiveness in those women who are, for any reason, predisposed to it.

The more outwardly aggressive men and women are, the less self-destructive they are, and *vice versa*. Thus, if women in our society were really free to direct their aggressive drives creatively one would expect self-destructiveness among them to be low, which is not the case.

It is difficult to see how self-destructiveness or self-destructive behaviour could be inherited directly, but a propensity for it may well be. Babies vary greatly, not only in physical constitution but also in psychological make-up. Some people are probably born vulnerable and with tendencies to become self-destructive if experience, particularly early experience, pushes them that way. Others are born resilient and strong and tend to deal with difficulties or unpleasant situations in a different way.

Another way in which heredity influences self-destructiveness is in the way it does, or does not, match the individual to the environment in which he is raised. Mismatch in this respect leads to frustration and often to anxiety, and these are the bases of self-destructiveness. A gifted child born into an insensitive and unstimulating family will experience much frustration. A slow-learning or average child in a gifted family will also experience frustration and anxiety, and sensitivity on the part of the parents may not be sufficient to avert disaster.

It seems probable that most, perhaps all, human beings are programmed to behave self-destructively under some circumstances. Many can be conditioned in childhood to behave self-destructively for the rest of their lives, either in all circumstances or in circumstances which would not drive most people to self-destructiveness. Qualities such as vulnerability, instability, stamina or a strong or weak will to survive when things are difficult may well be the result of interaction between heredity and early environment. These qualities, or lack of them, make up the kind of temperament that tends easily towards self-destructiveness in certain environments.

Thus self-destructive behaviour is probably not basic to human behaviour. It is more a potentiality which is developed from conflict or confusion in restricted situations which are not supported from outside and from which there seems to be no escape. The resulting anger, frustration and sense of hopelessness can have a number of results, some of them self-destructive. To give a simple analogy, if one's knowledge of languages is restricted to English then, as long as one remains in an English-speaking country, one is, linguistically speaking, under no pressure and is wholly supported by the environment, so that one is probably not even conscious of any restriction. But if one were suddenly to find oneself in an environment where only Chinese was spoken, or in which it was necessary to speak a number of languages, the linguistic environment would no longer be supportive and one would be under some pressure in matters of communication. As a result, one would feel frustrated. If there was no opportunity to learn the new languages or if one felt unable to do so (one might for instance, believe that it would be impossible to do so), one would feel that there was no escape and might then take to drink or some other form of self-destruction. In such a situation failure to make every effort to learn the other languages would itself be a form of self-destructiveness.

An even more striking example is if one had to live in a world where no English was spoken and yet one's immediate environment, particularly one's family or mother, had been wholly geared to teaching one English, perhaps insisting that English be the only language spoken and even threatening punishment, or withdrawal of love, if one did not comply. After this, when faced with the outside world, one would be in a state of dilemma, and probably confusion, and in danger of behaving self-destructively.

Many patterns of behaviour are like languages. One absorbs them from one's parents. One modifies or extends them by contact with the outside world. Discrepancy between the two is stressful and frustrating.

This basic pattern of restriction and support, or lack of it, can be seen in many aspects of life and at all ages. For instance, a small girl who has been unsuccessful in her efforts to stay up late or to persuade her mother to buy sweets may bang her head against the wall or throw away her favourite toy in anger and frustration. A schoolgirl who does not understand the subject she studies, or who feels that she has little chance of passing a forthcoming examination, may stop work altogether and throw away her books in despair, thereby bringing about the very situation she fears. A girl with a severe physical handicap reached the age of eighteen and had to leave the close, supporting school for disabled children where she had lived in a loving atmosphere from the age of five. She found that the outside world had little use for a crippled young woman and that it offered little support. After two years of misery and frustration she killed herself. So did a middle-aged business woman whose security was lost when she realized that she faced financial ruin and charges of fraud. A young wife gave up her job because her husband wanted her only to cook and clean for him, then found that the days were boring and empty and found herself increasingly resentful, nagging and fearful that he would not return home from work at the earliest possible moment. A woman of sixty, widowed after forty years of emotional dependence on her husband, found herself unable to make a new life. The future seemed bleak and without hope. She took to drink.

In a restricting and frustrating situation self-destructiveness may be a choice made from moral principles, particularly in those motivated by ideals. A good example of this is Captain Oates' suicide. He was under pressure in that he feared that if he remained alive, the whole party would die. He therefore decided on a self-destructive course and walked out into the blizzard to his death. His apparent self-destructiveness was a moral act, designed to save his companions. This type of self-destructiveness is rare, as is the type of suicide that is offered under certain circumstances, usually in wartime, in which people operating behind enemy lines are issued with 'suicide capsules', to take if they are captured to avoid the horrors of torture and the possibility of giving vital information to the enemy while undergoing it. Occasionally a situation may be so extreme that the continuation of life may be more self-destructive than the ending of it. An example of this might be the simultaneous suicides, in prison, of three members of the Baader-Meinhof gang, when they realized that the plan to free them had failed. They would presumably not have killed themselves had escape still seemed possible.

These types of suicide do not come within the scope of this book as they are not self-destructive in the sense in which it is used here.

In sharp contrast to these circumstantial forms of self-destructiveness is the kind that is almost entirely internal, stemming from feelings and fantasies which are themselves likely to be the result of an earlier, frustrating environment. Some people who seem to have everything they could wish for and every opportunity to make what they can of their lives, with no external pressures or restrictions, pursue an unremittingly self-destructive course and may kill themselves.

Most self-destructive people come somewhere between these two extremes. Under extreme conditions most people can be self-destructive and most are vulnerable to certain situations. In observing self-destructive behaviour one usually finds a combination of external and internal factors. Thus a young mother stuck at home with small babies may become depressed and unable to enjoy her children, or even to care for them. Another may manage the house-work and the babies but overdo household tasks with such frenetic activity that no time is left for self-development or for doing things with the children. Many women who are frustrated by loveless or otherwise difficult marriages and who can see no escape from them, often take to drink or self-poisoning or other forms of self-destructiveness.

Sometimes the external situation is more subtle. Although the frustration comes from outside, often from pressure imposed by parents or husband or financial problems, the inability to escape lies in the woman's personality. A sixteen-year-old girl was good at school work although not interested in it. She was pushed by ambitious parents to do well in examinations and be a credit to them by going to university. She had no desire to do this but felt unable to go against their wishes. Instead she developed severe anxiety and sleeplessness so that she was unable to go to school or to do anything else. A girl of twenty-one was serious in her hopes of success as a fashion model but was under continual pressure from her parents to leave London, return home to a small town and work as a shop girl.

She was determined to stay in London and try to make her own way, but the resulting conflicts were powerful and she began to take drugs. She became unreliable and her drug habits impaired her career which led her to take more drugs. Had she given way to her parents and returned home she would have had support from them, but her frustrations would have come from the limited opportunities for her chosen career, in which they did not support her.

Sometimes the frustrating situation has become completely internal, often due to a longstanding lack of something that was essential to development; perhaps understanding, a close, sensitive relationship or freedom. There are many young people who appear to have many opportunities open to them yet make no progress, lack motivation and indulge in self-destructive behaviour such as drug-taking, self-poisoning or self-starvation, failing exams or refusal to participate or to explore possibilities. Many of these young people have suffered some kind of lifelong deprivation, often from mothers who are themselves neurotic or depressed, or powerful parents whose own equilibrium has depended on keeping control of their children or setting up their own fantasies among them.

Self-destructive behaviour often occurs when the situation is no longer externally frustrating or when escape is theoretically possible. A woman brought up to traditional rôles, who has never had any ambition to be anything other than a wife and mother, may find that society and her husband no longer support her in these exclusive rôles. She may need to work for financial reasons, or when her children leave home she may find that life has little to offer and society is no longer so sympathetic to the 'little woman' performing only traditional duties at home. Yet her whole being and background rebels against the idea of further development or increased independence. Such a woman is particularly vulnerable in the modern world and liable to react with depression or another self-destructive activity. She may turn to a kind of self-destructiveness that is strongly manipulative, such as illness or threats of suicide, which aims to keep her husband or children at home. This is often a wild attempt to retain or restore the supportive environment which she feels she is losing and without which she cannot continue to function in her accustomed manner. Thus self-destructiveness often appears when the restricted situation is no longer supported by the environment. The ability to take advantage of a changing environment and the opportunities it offers depends on the ability to appreciate the new situation and to impose oneself on it. Many women are unable to do this and are still being brought up to be unable to do it.

Sometimes self-destructiveness appears because the escape route itself, though clear, is insufficiently supported by the environment. Thus a woman may long for new activities and experiences and see exactly what she would like to do, yet be prevented by a controlling husband or else by the sheer impossibility of surviving in what she wants to do, especially if her escape is contrary to the customs of the society in which she lives.

Self-destructiveness can have a positive, even beneficial, result, particularly when it occurs as an attempt to escape from a situation that seems impossible and not from the difficulties of choice. The self-destructive behaviour may change the situation or reveal a new way of dealing with it, and thus actually lead to achievement. George Pickering discusses this subject in his interesting book *Creative Malady*. Florence Nightingale rejected the traditional female rôle at first rebelliously and later, in an apparently self-destructive way, by taking to her bed. In fact this retreat into illness was the only way in which she could achieve what she felt she must achieve, the organization of nursing services. Mary Baker Eddy behaved hysterically and self-destructively until this very behaviour led her into the 'revelation' which caused her to form and lead the Christian Science movement. Sometimes self-destructiveness can be a time of waiting until something helpful turns up. An example of this was Elizabeth Barrett Browning, a chronic invalid and drug-taker until Robert Browning came into her life. Unlike many other self-destructive persons, she recognized where her true interests lay and was able to elope with him to a better life away from the tyranny of her father. (It must be said, however, that difficulties in her personality persisted for the rest of her life.)

The origins of self-destructiveness always lie partly in the personality, and self-destructiveness is profoundly influenced by personal and internal matters. Not all the imprisoned members of the Baader-Meinhof gang killed themselves after the Mogadishu raid, and one of them (Irmgard Möller) made a suicidal gesture and survived. Not all young women in Victorian times who longed for a different way of life or who were tyrannized by their fathers retreated into illness. No matter how frustrating and restricting a situation is or has been, not everyone reacts with self-destructiveness and, of those who do, each is self-destructive in her own way. Those who are self-destructive in the face of intolerable and inescapable external frustrations are often those of a strong personality and ability and they are often actually stronger and healthier and they achieve more than those who comply. Examples are Captain Oates and Florence Nightingale. This is one reason why the person who becomes a psychiatric patient is sometimes the healthiest member of their family.

On the other hand those who are self-destructive in situations of opportunity and choice, or in situations from which there is clearly an escape, are usually those whose self-esteem is low. They feel guilty, unworthy and of no importance. Since people tend to try to make the external reality of their lives conform to their fantasies about themselves, they proceed to behave in a manner which shows the world how unworthy or blameworthy they are.

Self-esteem, or lack of it, is of great importance in matters of achievement and failure. First there is the self-esteem, or lack of it, that comes from parents and family, of feeling that one is, or is not, a valuable person in one's own right and not a liability or merely an appendage to one's parents. Second is the self-esteem that comes from the outside world where, for women, success after puberty is most likely to be seen as the display of traditional virtues, passivity, good homemaking and being sexually attractive, now combined with the new awareness of themselves as people in their own right. These different kinds of self-esteem, or lack of it, can interact violently to mould the adult woman into what she becomes, and can change and affect her in later life, too. Such clashes and inconsistencies tend to be greater in women than in men in our society, and this probably contributes to the low self-esteem which underlies so much of their failure and self-destructiveness.

Self-destructiveness is encouraged by such character traits as dependency, passivity, manipulativeness and perfectionism. These are not in themselves self-destructive, but they tend to become so. These characteristics are interdependent and usually co-exist, often with other forms of self-destructiveness. All are closely related to lack of personal development and, in particular, to lack of self-esteem and a poor sense of self.

Women's achievements in our time include choice and opportunity. Despite a number of important exceptions, women have more choice and more opportunity today than ever before in the history of the world. Today a woman can choose to be educated, earn a good wage, train for a profession, and devote her life to that profession or not, as she wishes. She can choose to remain unattached and be wholly respectable in so doing. Without incurring social rejection she can live alone and support herself on the same pay as a man, she can live with a man to whom she is not married, have children and raise them alone or with anyone she chooses, change her partners as often as she likes, or choose to live with another woman. Or she can opt for the traditional rôle, find a man to support her and whom she can serve, and devote herself entirely to him and to housekeeping and raising children. In a way that was never possible before she can choose whatever mode of life she desires.

Yet whether or not these are seen as choices by any individual woman depends very much on the opinion of those among whom she lives. There is no longer universal pressure of public opinion about these matters, and different groups exert pressure in different ways. This leads to conflict and difficulty for many women.

Although women have achieved choice and opportunity, these are all too often pseudo-choice and sham opportunity. Sometimes the reasons are failure of the Equal Opportunity Act, some action or attitude of male chauvinism, or simply that opportunity and choice have come too late. More frequently, the cause lies in the woman herself and in the way she has been brought up. In our present world of choice the majority of women are not educated to make choices, do not wish to choose, and frown on their sisters who do. The fact that there is so much choice either frightens them consciously or drives them to hide from it and try to find a way of life that ignores choice. This in itself is a form of self-destructiveness.

This is an important reason why women tend to be more self-destructive than men in our society. But have they always been so? History and literature are full of self-destructive men, but then history and literature are mostly about or by men, and self-destructive women do appear. One of the earliest was Jocasta, mother of Oedipus, who married her son (surely in itself a self-destructive act), and then hanged herself. Erigone killed herself from grief and Athenian women began to copy her. Boadicea took poison rather than face defeat. Juliet's self-destructive passion for her family's enemy led to her suicide. Madame Bovary destroyed her relationships and other people's peace of mind. Elizabeth Barrett Browning was forced by her father into a self-destructive rôle and became an invalid addicted to opium. Anna Karenina, trapped in a loveless marriage by a rigid society, took refuge in her self-destructive relationship with Vronsky which ended in her suicide. In Victorian times young ladies languished with a strange wasting disease called *green anaemia* or *chlorosis,* which does not exist today and is thought to have been self-induced or fictitious. In our own time girls who are in conflict with themselves and their families tend to suffer from *anorexia nervosa* or self-starvation.

Self-destructiveness has probably been with us as long as civilization, but in women it has probably never been as widespread or as undermining as it is today. This is probably largely due to the rapid changes that are taking place in our time and to the loss of certainty in so many areas of life. Moreover, our age offers women unparalleled opportunities not only for fulfilment but also for self-destructiveness, and much of this is hidden or disguised. The present epidemics among women of suicidal gesture, wrist slashing, drug

dependence, anorexia nervosa and depression, are only the tip of the
iceberg. I believe that this great increase in self-destructiveness in
women comes partly from their increased opportunities, for in the
days when a woman had few opportunities she was more likely to
remain constricted by her position and to live a restricted though not
destructive life within those external restrictions. Now that so many
of the restrictions have been removed, and the traditional rôles of
daughter, wife and mother are no longer regarded as total or lifelong,
it is up to her to make what she can of her life. Many women, even
when they are aware of their limited lives, are unable to develop and
make use of available opportunities and so become passively, and
sometimes actively, self-destructive.

Each stage of a woman's life and each rôle that she plays has its
own patterns of self-destructiveness, and each of these is much
influenced by her personality. Different self-destructive patterns are
likely to be found in say, a girl in early adolescence, a student, a career
woman, a young mother tied down at home by babies, a single
woman, a childless woman, and a woman who finds that her children are now free of her or that her marriage has broken up, and a
widow. Also the type of self-destructiveness and often whether it
exists or shows at all, varies enormously not only with age and
circumstances, but also with social background and individual personality. Everyone fills certain rôles more easily and happily than
others. Some women are excessively strained by, say, the demands
of education, self-development or an active career. Others find the
restrictions of traditional rôles of wife and mother intolerably
restricting, or impossible to reconcile or combine with other things
they feel they need to do, yet they still have an overwhelming need to
be wives and mothers and if they do not achieve this they are
unhappy and unfulfilled.

Our society, while offering greater opportunities to women than
ever before, actually encourages self-destructiveness in them. The
traditional rôle of women is becoming self-destructive and the new
ways and new ideas encourage self-destructiveness, make it harder
not to be self-destructive, and also bring out latent self-
destructiveness which, in another setting, would never surface.
Many women still need traditional rôles, yet often find that these do
not provide the support enjoyed by former generations. Maintaining
a traditional rôle is now often just a means of hiding from reality in a
changing world and an excuse for lack of courage or failure to
develop. Yet traditional rôles are still needed and often need to be
combined with new rôles, with which they tend to conflict. In this
conflict relationships with husbands and children suffer most, often
catastrophically. And, because self-destructiveness is basically a

question of individual personality, the children suffer and the seeds of self-destructiveness are sown in the next generation. As we shall see, mothers in our society have an exceptionally difficult time, and as a result their children suffer.

Chapter Two

Achievement and Choice

Before we can decide why women succeed or fail we must have an idea of what we mean by success and failure. Success and failure are here defined not in a worldly sense but in relation to how people feel about themselves. Success is a sense of making good with what one has, perhaps making the best of what one has. Being successful means being good enough in what one does or has to do, and deciding what is 'good enough' involves subjective judgment. There also has to be realistic appraisal, both internal and external, in which an individual's feelings and fantasies are linked to the external world. Subjective satisfaction that lacks realistic appraisal is often achieved only by denial of reality. Success in the eyes of the world has no meaning if the process or the product brings no sense of satisfaction. A sense of achievement and realistic judgment are both essential to success.

Paradoxically, it is probably easier for women to be successsful in this sense in a world where virtually their only choice is traditional womanhood than in a world in which they are faced with much choice and in which they have aspirations of equal opportunity with men. In a traditional society those unsuited to the traditional rôle may escape or flounder, but the majority have the satisfaction of doing well what they feel they were meant to do or at least of making the best of a bad job to which there is no alternative.

In failure, the opposite of success, there is little or no sense of making good. There is lack of motivation, a sense of futility and an inability to use, and often even to recognize, opportunities. In failure discontent pervades. There is little or no sense of achievement.

For women in the western world today there is still a strong tradition demanding that women do their duty and make the best of it. But it is no longer a universal tradition. Our society no longer supports the old way of life in the way that it did. This lack of support for a continuing tradition brings choice and hence conflict to many women. What would have been success in the past now often lacks the sense of achievement. It is difficult to feel a sense of achievement in coping with difficulties and miseries if others think you brought them on yourself or could choose to step out of them altogether, and if you are incapable of choice the conflict may be intolerable. Yet in practice many women still feel that they have no choice. Thus old success tends to become new failure.

For an individual, achievement is doing something that brings satisfaction to the doer. Essentially it is making or renewing connections within oneself or with the outside world. It may be as simple as having a baby or making something or earning some money, but usually it is more complicated. It may be making or creating, learning and improving, acquiring and practising new skills, or becoming involved in what one does. It is setting goals and moving towards them. A sense of achievement comes from building relationships, the exercise of choice and self-expression, and from new understanding, a sense of quality, and a feeling of making progress. Achievement can be the satisfaction of curiosity, the relief from tension, the overcoming of difficulties, the sense of mastery, involvement and excitement, including intellectual excitement. It can be physical, sensual, emotional, intellectual or spiritual.

Achievement, however, can be false or perverse. What may seem to be achievement in the eyes of others may seem futile or disappointing to the doer. Or the goal may be false, perhaps acquisition for its own sake, or hurting or destroying oneself or others, the pursuit of false gods, the exercise of self-righteousness. It may simply be smugness. There is also the false achievement of compliance, simply doing things because they are expected of us rather than for any personal satisfaction. As we shall see, compliance is particularly hazardous for women today. Compliance can produce true achievement only in a highly structured social system which offers little choice, such as an army, a totalitarian régime, or a society strongly controlled by rigid customs.

Lack of achievement or achievement that is false or perverse leads to alienation, depression and a sense of futility. That these are so widespread today is one of our big problems.

A sense of achievement is probably basic to humans. It stems from feelings of satisfaction and reduction of tension which we may well share with lower animals. It can be seen in an infant mastering techniques such as walking, talking, and acquiring other skills. It can also be seen in children playing. A great deal of work has now been done on the sex differences in children's play and in the way children are encouraged to play. It may well be that some of the seeds of some women's destructiveness lie here. In simple situations and societies a sense of achievement is usually equivalent to getting on with life, or with what has to be done and is not a subject for doubt or debate. The traditional woman's rôle has been to grow up in the accepted feminine way, find (or be found) a suitable husband, and raise children. As long as she did this, she succeeded, and most did. Probably some women have always rebelled and found satisfaction in other ways, but this was rare. Lady Hester Stanhope, Mary Wollstonecraft and Florence Nightingale all rebelled against the traditional rôle, but such women were few. Many more women rebelled in a more traditional way, by influencing men, which brings its own sense of achievement.

Nowadays there is no generally accepted rôle for women, or, indeed, for men. There are wide differences both in individuals and in different sections of the community. Some sections of society cling to traditional ideas or try to create new rôles, others accept recent changes. No one fits everywhere, and many attempts to find new rôles turn into the impossible situation of trying to be every-thing at once, or else into confusion amid multiple and incompatible expectations.

What have women achieved in our time?

Firstly, women have achieved, and are still achieving, knowledge and feelings about their rights and increased awareness of them-selves. Unless their eyes and ears are closed, which sometimes they make sure they are, women cannot fail to know that they now have rights which they did not have before, that they can be individuals as much as men, that they can choose their future lives much more easily than formerly, and that along with this there is a great deal of pressure to keep them where they were or where men think they ought to be in a male-dominated society, and where many women still think they should be. Furthermore, awareness tends to diminish respect for authority, and also for given values. Although this means opportunity for many, it is also a loss and a threat. There is loss of certainty and loss of support, two things that were important to women's traditional rôle. Many women felt more secure in being certain that they were the weaker sex than in being aware that they are not.

Secondly women have gained, and are still gaining, opportunity for individual achievement. Achievement, in the sense of doing things that bring satisfaction to the doer, is the only tolerable basis of life. In other ages and societies this kind of feeling would be more likely to come from 'doing one's duty', or unconsciously following a prescribed path or even simply keeping out of trouble. Nowadays women who try to keep going by following traditional, prescribed paths, or who allow themselves to be driven into them, are not supported by public opinion in the way they used to be and like men,

most women need to find satisfaction through their own achievements.

Opportunity for individual achievement and satisfaction means
choice, and choice is perhaps the greatest achievement of women so
far. There is choice in education and training. There are the Equal
Opportunity and the Equal Pay Acts. There is choice in sexual
matters, and even choice of a sexual partner's sex, which can be made
public. There is choice in marriage, and whether to marry or not
without the strong social pressures that existed formerly. Women
can marry, cohabit, share their lives with whom they like for as long
as they like, or remain single if they prefer and move in circles where
they can do this without ridicule or opprobrium. They can choose to
work in whatever field they choose to train, or they can choose not to
work and to live on social security. They can choose to have children
when they desire them, married or not, or to remain childless. There
is another range of choices that can be made once the children are
grown and a woman has perhaps thirty or forty years of active life
ahead. The second half of life is not only likely to be much longer
than ever before but is also open to achievement in a way it never was
before. Yet, if she so wishes, a woman can still choose a traditional
woman's life and be exclusively a wife and mother. Many still
choose it. But the difference is that it is now, at least in theory, a
positive choice and no longer brings the satisfactions of coping with
the inevitable or doing one's duty.

Thus one of the biggest changes for women in our time is the
ability, and often the necessity, to choose. For in former times, unless
she was outstanding or exceptionally rebellious, a woman had little
or no choice. Nowadays, if she is skilled at choosing and can balance
what she chooses against real possibilities, she is probably much
better off than her forbears. But at the present time it is in dealing
with choice that many women find their greatest difficulties.

Choice means loss of control by others. It also often means loss of
control *of* others, for if we concentrate on controlling, there is no
room left for choice. All forms of loss of control can be frightening.
Nowadays, a woman who becomes exclusively a wife and mother
chooses to be this and no one forces her into the rôle. But the
existence of choice can be a great difficulty. As long as one feels part
of a system and acts as that system dictates, one is less likely to feel a
failure, alienated, futile and depressed. An example of such a situation, and not just for women, is the army into which many people are
conscripted during wartime. Most function contentedly in the army
for the duration of war, some are happier than ever before, but many
afterwards find that they are lost, without direction and lacking in
motivation, and many of these are the best soldiers. People who are

trained to have no choice find choice difficult. In the past women have been conditioned from birth for their traditional rôle and have tended to accept this without thought of alternatives. Men have always had more choice and for them choice grew slowly as society became more complex and more flexible.

So in a way choice is women's greatest achievement. The conflict that comes from choice is the price they have to pay. What are the particular conflicts of women today?

Conflicting most markedly with women's recent achievements are traditional ideas of woman as wife, mother, and sex symbol. Whatever else they may do, most women have and need these traditional rôles. Many men still demand them. Women are liberated in how they pass the time, in the professions they follow and in the interests they pursue, but many still desire or feel it necessary to cope totally with household and children and also to play the rôle of desirable wife, greeting the husband's evening homecoming with everything prepared. These are often the wives of the most success-ful and desired men. Such a woman may have a satisfying life and job but will, without hesitation, give up everything she has achieved because her husband wishes to move elsewhere, or even because he wants her to have a baby which she will then have to look after. She may love the man more than the life she has built for herself and she may give up her own way of life without question, though often at heavy cost to herself. Some women are so set on performing these ⌄ rôles that a life of their own is unthinkable. It is still not uncommon for a man to treat his wife as his property and to demand, and refuse, his permission for anything outside her traditional rôle. I recently met a wife who could not even go to language classes in the after-noons because her husband was afraid she might make friends there, and he wanted her to stay at home in the afternoons in case he felt like telephoning her from the office. Such women tend to feel useless and depressed, particularly when their children have left home.

Further conflict comes from the difficulties of coping with what has been achieved. New opportunities bring new anxieties. Many women know what they want to do, or at least that they want to do something, yet they feel guilty and uncertain and are unable to pursue their own desires.

Still more conflict comes from the imperfections of what has been achieved and the difficulties of taking up new opportunities. These opportunities often exist in theory more than in practice and, when they do exist, are not what they seemed, or produce hidden difficul-ties or unexpected losses. Often wrong choices have been made which cannot afterwards be rectified. A woman who believes in equality of opportunity is likely to find her opportunities far from equal and her path blocked by tradition and by opposition, not only from men but often from women too.

For the majority of women the conflicts centre on men friends, husbands and children and the difficulties of reconciling their needs and demands with their own personal lives. Most women are probably aware of multiple sets of conflicting expectations which are difficult, and often impossible, to reconcile.

Conflict which is not resolved tends to lead to self-destructiveness. In desperation the sufferer turns against herself, feeling that she cannot cope or is inadequate or somehow blameworthy. Women have little tradition of conflict, and even today are not usually brought up and trained in a manner that is helpful in dealing with it. So the great increase in choice, and therefore of conflict, for women in recent years makes them vulnerable to self-destructiveness, which has become the scourge of women.

Self-destructiveness is a result of unresolved conflict. The conflict may be immediate or left over from the past. Conflicts of childhood, often over parents or independence, remain in the mind and tend to be reproduced in adult life.

Self-destructiveness denies the future. It perpetuates unhappiness and confusion from the past, even where it seeks to destroy it. It prevents growth and progress. It often has an underlying cause which may in itself be progressive though it seldom furthers this cause or improves the quality of life. Usually it is not deliberate but is an unconscious reaction to circumstances that may lie far in the past or to an impossible situation in the present. It can be purposeful and manipulative. It is an aberrant solution to problems or an attempt to escape from them. Often, and luckily, it is only a temporary phase. Few people go through life without ever being self-destructive.

Increased opportunities lead to increased self-destructiveness. It is up to each woman to make what she can of her life. Yet many women are unable to develop and make use of available opportunities. Thus the difficulties of choice can turn potential success into self-destructiveness.

Self-destructiveness, like achievement, is an individual reaction within a social situation.

Chapter Three

Society

During recent years, apart from social changes and new legislation which affect women directly, many other influences have affected achievement and self-destructiveness in women. The first of these is rapid change itself.

Superficial change can be a means of respite or inspiration, perhaps in the form of a holiday or a new job. It can also be an escape from reality and conflict, for example in a woman who buys a new dress or seeks a change of scene whenever life does not suit her. But people find it difficult to cope with change that affects what they feel to be their roots or the sources of their security. This is what tends to happen with the accelerating rate of social change which has been taking place in our time. Thus, it creates many difficulties. We cannot confidently expect to lead much the same life as did our parents and we know that our chidren's lives are likely to be different from ours. Rapid change requires the capacity to change oneself and also to prepare one's children for further, as yet unpredictable, change. The unpredictability of the future, like the new opportunities open to women, leads to feelings of loss of control and loss of self-confidence. Coping with change requires powers of observation, initiative, flexibility and endurance such as would not be needed if one could expect to lead much the same life with the same beliefs as one's forbears.

All change demands an appropriate level of personal development suitable to age and circumstances. Change can be difficult and threatening even in infancy. For example, an infant can be upset by a change of environment, a change in those caring for it, or even changing from a bottle to a cup or from a cot to a bed. To change successfully from the process of being educated to taking part in the world of work, from being single to being married, from being childless to being a mother and from being a needed mother to a mother with adult children, all require appropriate levels of development. But the changes that are taking place in our society are much greater than in former times and they are also different in kind. Life no longer consists of a series of predictable personal changes through which one can follow in the footsteps of one's mother and grandmother, keeping to the beliefs of one's ancestors. Each of us now has to work out each step for herself. Many women, either through training or temperament, are ill-equipped to do this.

In our society, in contrast to others less developed or more controlled, it is necessary to reach an advanced stage of personal development in order to survive, thrive and guard against the problems and vicissitudes of normal life. This is particularly true of women because of their new choices and new uncertainty. The failure or the inability to develop sufficiently to cope with this new choice and uncertainty is the root of much self-destructiveness. Many people survive and some thrive without achieving this development, but they are not only lucky they are also vulnerable. Changes in their lives, or problems that require advanced personal development, are liable to topple them into some form of self-destructiveness. As time goes on they are increasingly at risk. Many of the institutions in our society have traditionally supported undeveloped individuals and enabled them to lead easy, controlled, and even comfortable lives, but these are changing rapidly. Examples are marriage and sexual relationships, work and career prospects, and the upbringing and education of children and young people. It is no longer so easy to fit in and keep quiet. 'Adjustment' is no longer as worthy an aim as it used to be because one now has to discover or decide what one is going to adjust to, and so 'adjustment' is no longer so satisfying. There is unprecedented choice, often combined with immense frustration. If our source of security lies in doing as our parents did, we are in for a hard time. There are now new problems, prospects and horizons, together with new boundaries and loss of old boundaries, and, as individuals we have to cope with them. We can only cope if we are sufficiently developed. 'Appropriateness' has become more relevant than 'adjustment'.

Developing in this way is of course not new. Many people in the past, especially those who broke from their backgrounds, have developed sufficiently to impose themselves on new environments and have made new lives of their own, quite different from the lives of their parents. But these were mostly people who chose to go against the main stream. In other words they deliberately chose to choose, to break away from established rôles and to do what was not expected of them. This is different from having to choose. Unwilling refugees always have a hard time. Yet most of us are now refugees from the past, willingly or unwillingly.

It now seems appropriate to examine some of the major changes

that have been and are taking place in order to see how they affect
women.

One of the biggest changes during the century has been in health.
Physically we are healthier than ever before. A hundred years ago
one adult in three died of an infectious disease. In most families
several children died before they were grown, and many lost their
mothers from childbirth or disease before the family was complete.
But major infections, nutritional diseases and the big killers of
mothers and children are now conquered. During the last fifty years,
for the first time in history, parents have been able to have confidence
in the survival of their children. Families are now more likely to be
broken up by divorce than by death. Even the loss of a single child in
a family is unusual, and the death of a mother from infection or in
childbirth has become extremely rare. Moreover, although the death
rate in middle age is still higher than it need be, we have come to
expect that we shall live on into old age. If we take adult life as
starting at the age of sixteen, we can reasonably expect to have sixty
years of healthy adult life and, with today's small families, we are
likely to spend no more than ten of those years pregnant or looking
after pre-school children and perhaps another ten running a busy
home. There remains for most of us forty or fifty years of adult life to
be lived. This is a great change from the days, still within living
memory, when a woman was likely to spend twenty-five years in
pregnancy and childbearing and, if she survived that, probably had
only a few more years with her growing children. Our grandmothers, if they believed, as most did, that they had no function in
life other than to keep house and family and to bear and rear children,
were supported in this belief by their environment until they died.
But many modern women with such beliefs feel frustrated and
trapped when they discover the long years that lie ahead. A woman
now has to decide what she wants to do with them. She may be
unable, because of her upbringing, training, or temperament, to
make this decision. Even if she knows what she wants circumstances
may make it impossible to put into practice. Her long years of
physical health and theoretical freedom may turn into long years of
mental ill-health and hopelessness. Thus improved health can actually lead to self-destructiveness.

In this connection it is interesting to note that although the majority of serious diseases have been conquered, the amount of 'illness'
has increased, and much of this is in women. There has been a change
in the types of illness that are most common. Where before a patient
went to the doctor with symptoms and the doctor could usually
make a diagnosis on visible physical signs, nowadays a much higher
proportion of illnesses consist of symptoms only, and the doctor has

to rely on what the patient says she feels. In huge numbers of cases there are no physical signs and the symptoms do not tally with physical diseases. The doctor has to take the patient's word that she is ill, and any physical tests he makes are likely to have negative or irrelevant results. These 'functional' diseases have always been with us, but doctors see many more of them nowadays. There are also many diseases whose signs the doctor can see for himself but which clearly fluctuate according to the patient's state of mind and what is happening at home. These include asthma, a variety of rashes, tremors, and many stomach and bowel disorders. In recent years there has been discussion in medical journals about the 'epidemic' of neurosis and psychosomatic illness that has arisen in recent years. Much of it is in women struggling with their frustrations and conflicts, many of which have arisen because of the changes in our society.

When these problems assail the mothers of young children, they influence the next generation and are often repeated in it. Depression, neurosis, and psychosomatic disorders among mothers responsible for children in their formative years set the scene for self-destructiveness in the next generation. To grow up with a depressed, frustrated or neurotic mother is a common tragedy in our age.

Another big change for women has been in education. Although it cannot yet be said that there is full equality for women, and there are still many deficiencies, we now have many thousands of highly educated women and, in some areas, a tradition of higher education that goes back more than a century. This helps greatly towards a productive life and the ability to make use of opportunities. A good education provides the background and qualifications necessary for women to succeed and enjoy themselves in the world of work, and also resources and sources of satisfaction to women who are tied to the home or unable to participate in wider activities. Education therefore can mitigate against the self-destructiveness that comes from the restrictions of personality and opportunities which are still the lot of many women. A good education can enable a woman to find what really satisfies her and give her the skill to achieve it. Education enables a woman to make a good life, helps her through years of inevitable restriction, and makes a valuable contribution to whatever she wants or needs to do.

Education, however, also creates difficulties. Women accustomed to intellectual work are sometimes frustrated by the inevitability of housework, nappy-washing and the unremitting conversation of small children, and find that they are ill-equipped to cope with these matters. However much she loves her children, if some of her essential interests are elsewhere, as they usually are in an educated woman, her children are liable to suffer, especially if she is also frustrated. Most women wish for homes and families, but the difficulties may be overwhelming. These include the strain on a woman and the physical fatigue of trying to cope with a family as well as doing that for which she has been trained and which has become part of her essential being. Women are not on the whole trained to lead double lives, but most of them have to lead them and, with the increase in working mothers, more and more do this. In spite of the increasing domestication of men, it is still true that however hard a woman works and however much she earns, it is still likely that in terms of physical and mental work she carries far more of the burden of the household and the children than does her husband. In such a situation she may sometimes become self-destructive because the burden is too great. Part of her is bound to suffer and it is impossible for her to be fulfilled. This also applies to less educated women who go out to work. It is one of the great problems of our society.

This leads to the question of sexual equality. We now have Acts of Parliament which grant equality in certain areas and there is much talk about it. But it is impossible to attain equality under the present, or perhaps under any, system. Moreover, emphasis on the idea of equality when this is not a reality can be frustrating. Prejudice against women, in both sexes, may diminish over the years, but it is still true that most women wish to be wives and mothers, and even ten years devoted predominantly to children means that in many fields, especially the highly skilled and most satisfying; women inevitably miss much of the experience that is essential for further progress and responsibility. For this reason alone, unless the experience of raising a family is of particular value to a chosen occupation, it is difficult to see how women can be equal with men unless our social system changes radically. The semblance and legality of equality without its reality is one of the frustrating situations for women in our society. Sometimes what is blamed on prejudice or male chauvinism is in fact due to inequality against which there can be no legislation and where it is difficult to see how there can be improvement except insofar as the husband is willing to share the disadvantages.

Another big change in women's lives has been brought about by the development of easy and effective methods of birth control, supported by abortion. Unless prevented by health, religion, or ignorance, which can themselves lead to frustration and self-destructive behaviour, women now have control over their bodies as far as pregnancy is concerned. This of course is immensely important to the women's movement and to the concept of women's liberation, but it has its darker, frustrating, side which can contribute to self-destructive tendencies. Since fertility declines with age, the deliberate postponement of pregnancy may lead to childlessness, which contributes to frustration and self-destructiveness. Furthermore, many women feel that pregnancy loses it spontaneity when it is planned and deliberate and they dislike a mechanistic attitude in having and rearing children. Some postpone pregnancy indefinitely or until it is too late. Some are unable to face the decision at all, perhaps doubting their own capacities as mothers or conscious of the contrast between the deliberacy of the decision and uncertainty of the outcome, or always feeling that the time is not yet right or the circumstances not yet perfect. Some know that they are unsuited to motherhood and although they may then, by avoiding pregnancy altogether, spare their children the burden of being born to unsuitable mothers, it does not always save the non-parent from self-destructiveness. Moreover there are women who, before these attitudes were common, had children for social reasons, because it was expected of them, and now openly or secretly regret having done so. All these feelings and attitudes turn easily into self-destructiveness.

There can also be much unhappiness and frustration over abortion. Because it is so easy to obtain many women feel that they are pushed into it by husbands or boyfriends, family or doctor. Many women who, because of poor adaptation, have self-destructive tendencies, suffer greatly as a result of abortion and it may form the focus of increasing self-destructiveness.

The sexual revolution of our day has been one of the most difficult changes for many women. We are all exposed to sexual matters much more extensively and in quite different ways from a generation ago. If we try to retain old values and beliefs then society no longer supports us and we fall easily into the combination of frustration, lack of support, and no escape that is the basis of self-destructiveness. The very fact that attitudes have changed so much removes the support provided by doing what one has been brought up to do and what one has always been told was right.

Our society, as revealed in what is said and done, tends to view sex in a changed moral context, outside a religious context, and often without reference to pregnancy or marriage. Sex has tended to become an end in itself, often part of a current, transient relationship or even solely as a matter of technique and achievement. It is not surprising that much self-destructive behaviour is found in sexual matters. Frigidity is a common way in which self-destructiveness is expressed, and so is promiscuity, 'cock-teasing' and preoccupation with sexual technique. Those who stick to more old-fashioned attitudes can easily find themselves self-destructive in this withholding. Refusal to participate can set up intolerable conflicts.

Within marriages and what are known as 'stable relationships' a multitude of different attitudes and actions are accepted. There is little set pattern for society as a whole except to some extent that of constancy as long as a relationship lasts. Some relationships, even in those who change partners frequently, are remarkably 'traditional' in pattern, with the man as dominant and the breadwinner who is served by the woman, and the woman as submissive and economically dependent, performing most of the chores. The arrival of children often accentuates this pattern and the woman, tied but conscious of the opportunities that in theory are open to her, may be driven into self-destructiveness, even though she may actively have sought and encouraged such a situation. Seeking a traditional form of relationship in an unsuitable context can itself be a form of self-destructiveness. Other relationships are more sharing, but the chief burden in practical matters still usually falls on the woman. Thus false situations tend to develop and the woman becomes frustrated and dissatisfied.

Along with the changes in sex have gone changes in marriage and in relationships akin to marriage. Marriage is still popular but has become less common and less expected. Relationships, both sexual and merely friendly, between men and women who are not married to each other have become more open and more acceptable. The divorce rate has risen rapidly and divorce has become easier. It is common and widely accepted that many people now go through their lives with a series of relationships, both in marriage and outside, each more or less exclusive while it lasts but not necessarily lasting for more than a few years or, especially with young people, months or weeks. All this is profoundly different from the traditional Christian view of marriage and the present climate of opinion can be threatening to those not acclimatized to it. People accumulate children, their own and their partners', and may then lose them. Stepsiblings and half-siblings come and go along with the step-parents. It can all be confusing and frustrating and, in those whose personal development is not attuned to it, it can provoke self-destructiveness. Labour-saving technology, particularly in food, clothing and household machinery, has done much for the liberation of women and, by freeing them from lengthy household tasks, enables them to do much more than formerly towards exploring opportunities and developing and practising other skills. But machines do not care for children or plan the running of a household. Most women have to do these things themselves, whatever else they may do.

It is perhaps when one comes to the question of children that one finds the greatest change simply because here is the least change, although everything else has changed. Babies and small children need care all the time, just as they have always done. The slow pace and the quiet, receptive sensitivity needed to raise healthy children is difficult to attain in our society and difficult to reconcile with everything else that goes on. Except in those who have a vocation for it, every influence seems to militate against it, and many who try to achieve it are sadly conscious of what they are missing in the outside world and are also aware of those parts of themselves that they are failing to develop. They are caught in a trap and whatever they do is self-destructive. This is one of the most powerful ways in which our society fosters self-destructiveness in women.

Lip service is paid to equality of opportunity and women are becoming aware of their potential. Lip service is also paid to the importance of the quiet and constant mothering of small children. Yet little is done to reconcile the conflicts and difficulties in these two things. Good mothering has become much more difficult and society provides little support. It does not even encourage the talents of those who are gifted in the care of small children, let alone cherish and foster this gift which is probably one of the most valuable and most needed of talents. The situation regarding young children today makes a mockery of much high-mindedness about women's rights and women's potentials. Moreover, by driving young mothers into self-destructiveness our society is damaging its own future by damaging the health and resilience of the next generation.

A few words must be said about male chauvinism, for this too is involved in changes. Male chauvinism is a new phrase with pejorative connotations, which refers to traditional male outlook and behaviour. Male chauvinism exists, often encouraged by women who hold traditional views of the relations between the sexes or who choose this as a shield against their own lack of development, so making it their own form of self-destructiveness. What used to be regarded as feminine and desirable in a woman, such as passivity, subservience and compliance, have, within our own time, become self-destructive, sometimes powerfully so. No longer overtly supported by a society that legislates for equal opportunity, these attitudes of dominance and subservience continue, often in the form of sadism and masochism, each nourishing the other in an endless cycle of destructiveness and self-destructiveness. Yet to lack 'traditional' virtues, passivity, subservience and compliance, is also widely regarded as undesirable. The most admired and successful woman is expected to have all the traditional virtues as well as the expected modern characteristics. Since this combination is virtually impossible, conflict ensues, and often also self-destructiveness.

Chapter Four

Personality

We have seen that social changes have combined to withdraw much of the support which society formerly gave to traditional womanhood and we have seen how women are now expected to show traditional virtues, while at the same time conforming to more modern pressures, for example to be attractive, sexy, thin, successful and rich. The result is confusing for many women and some, unable to see a way through the conflict, resort to self-destructiveness. We have also seen that in a society such as ours, which changes rapidly, women need a much higher level of personal development if they are to avoid becoming self-destructive. How far a particular woman resolves these conflicts constructively and how far she finds herself driven to destruction depends on her personality and on her individual situation. Many women whose level of personal development is low are kept from self-destructiveness by a particularly supportive environment. There are, for instance, still pockets of traditional life where social change is slow and people can absorb the values and ways of their parents and neighbours without conflict. There are also women who are protected from their own lack of development by fitting into a highly structured system of organization and absorbing its values. Such women are sometimes found in big organizations and in the civil service, or else married to servicemen, diplomats or executives. These women may even seem to be exceptionally stable and strong. The protection of the organization often makes up for personal weakness and deficiencies. There are also many women who are 'carried' through the complexities, change and conflicts of modern life by husbands who find personal satisfaction in performing this function. Others find their support in the raising of children, but such women may achieve their own stability only at the expense of their children. All such women, if the external support which enables them to carry on is withdrawn, or if it ceases to be adequate, tend to break down into some form of self-destructiveness. Thus such behaviour often occurs when a marriage collapses or when the children grow up. The only real protection women have today lies not in their supports but in themselves and in their own capacity for achievement.

By personality I mean everything a person is in herself and everything that makes her different from other people. The first essential in personal development is a sense of self, or 'real me', which means having a feeling about who and what one is and what one is not, together with a life that is lived according to that self. Without this feeling of 'real me' one is living in the shell rather than at the core of oneself. This may be satisfactory as long as the shell is fully supported by the environment. Thus, in a rigid society compliant people abound because they have had no need to develop. As long as they are supported by the environment they blend with it and are usually unaware of their compliance and lack of inner core. But as soon as the environment changes or fails such a person tends to lack motivation and finds life empty, stagnant, futile or unreal. Because our society is no longer rigid but changes rapidly and so is much less supportive to compliant personalities, a characteristic problem of our age is the 'identity crisis', which occurs typically in adolescence but can occur at any stage in life. Identity crises occur in those who, although they have some sense of self, find it insufficient for deciding their future way of life and imposing themselves on the changing environment. Before they can do these things they need to separate themselves from their parents, make relationships with people of their own age, develop sexual identity and work out their own moral values and aspirations. Most people emerge from identity crises with a strengthened sense of self. But sometimes the struggle ends in defeat and the individual retreats from his true self or erects an elaborate camouflage to conceal the fact that he is not in touch with himself and has little sense of 'real me'. This is a form of self-destructiveness.

This feeling of 'real me' is the basis of sound personal development. It is sometimes strongly, though always patchily, present from early childhood, but many people are not conscious of it until adolescence or later. They may not be aware of its lack until a difficulty or crisis occurs through which feelings of unreality, emptiness or futility come to the surface.

Self-respect, a feeling of one's own value, is part of the sense of 'real me' and is a measure of the degree of separation from parents that one has attained and the degree to which one's moral standards are one's own. Self-respect is essential to personal progress and love. One cannot love others or enjoy one's own life if one does not respect and care for oneself.

Yet many women lack this vital sense, and many lose it in the course of their lives. Without it there is always a tendency to demonstrate one's own worthlessness, both to oneself and to others. Many such women are not even aware of their own lack of self-respect, for they often drift into dependency, submissiveness, compliance and lack of confidence. Many are also aggressive, rebellious and manipulative, for if one has no self-respect one also lacks a powerful regulator of behaviour. Many people would like to indulge in extreme behaviour or have fantasies of doing so. It is their self-respect that holds them back.

A person with little self-respect often reduces it further because the ensuing behaviour is self-denigratory. This is why someone who begins to lose her self-respect is liable to deteriorate rapidly. An example was Christine, who never had a high opinion of herself. In order to carry on a normal life she needed much support and encouragement from her husband and family. She also tended to seek oblivion whenever problems loomed. When her husband was away on business she tended to drink heavily to get away from the problems of daily living and to blot out the long lonely evenings. The time came when her husband began an affair with another woman. Christine became depressed and drank more than ever. Her husband gave up his mistress and there was a reconciliation but Christine felt she could no longer trust him. She drank more and was drunk whenever there was a decision to be made or a problem to be solved. Although she had previously been a person who liked to keep up appearances, she now changed in this respect. She no longer kept her home clean or cared if friends and neighbours saw her drunk. She drank unashamedly in front of her children and would attack them if they tried to stop her. She bought drink instead of food so that her husband had to do the shopping for the family. When he managed to remove the drink from the house and cut off the funds to buy it, she searched the house for alcoholic substitutes and drank surgical spirit or scent. She even broke into a neighbour's house and stole a bottle of whisky. She could not wait until she reached her own house before drinking it and was found unconscious on the garden path.

Thelma felt she was nothing. She had a husband and two small children but could not believe that she was important to them. She suffered from bouts of tension that she found intolerable. When these came over her she would take drugs and rush out of the house, sometimes in her nightdress, leaving the children alone, and wander round the streets. In pubs she would pick up men and seemed to find temporary relief in sexual encounters of a casual and degraded nature. Several times she was beaten up and had to be admitted to hospital. Eventually she was found dead. The post-mortem examination revealed an overdose of drugs, but no one could say whether she had meant to kill herself.

Lack of self-respect and low self-esteem are common traits in women's personalities and are the source of many difficulties today. Although feelings of self-esteem probably originate in infancy and early childhood and are profoundly influenced by relationships within the family, particularly with parents, girls, on the whole, have more difficulty than boys in developing feelings of their own worth. This is often perpetuated from mother to daughter. A girl whose mother lacks self-esteem has special difficulty in acquiring her own, whereas her brothers are more likely to find models elsewhere. It is easier for a girl to develop a sense of her own worth if her mother has a strong sense of hers. This is probably why girls usually have few problems over this if their mothers are working women. Moreover, society's pressures on girls and the traditional training in submissiveness, passivity and dependency, which continues even today, do not develop self-esteem and tend to reduce it still further in those who are already deficient in it. Submissiveness, passivity and dependency increase compliance and are valuable in a patriarchal society where personal development in women tends to cause difficulties. But in a fast-changing society self-esteem is vital to psychological survival. Our society, while still demanding and praising traditional 'feminine' qualities, also demands quite different types of development and behaviour. These demands for impossible combinations lowers still further the self-esteem of those who feel unable to meet them. This vicious circle is the background to much self-destructive behaviour and is often a formidable barrier to any help or treatment.

People whose self-esteem is low tend to behave in a way which 'proves' that they are unworthy and this lowers their self-esteem still further. Periodic episodes of drunkenness is a common way in which certain women perpetuate this vicious circle. Another common form is seen in what I call the Doormat Syndrome. A woman feels that she only justifies her existence by enduring what others impose on her. Thus she is used and abused by all, particularly by those close to her, usually husband and children. She feels she has no escape and that it is essential to herself and to her family that she remains without assertion and without dignity. Even when asserting that she would like to escape and gain some self-respect she is unable to change or make any bid for personal freedom or dignity. Such a woman often retaliates in other ways, boosting herself with materialism or with competitiveness on behalf of her family, becoming excessively manipulative and subtly destructive of her husband and children, or else retreating into physical symptoms, depression or other psychiatric disorders, or into overtly self-destructive behaviour such as alcoholism or suicidal gesture, which are used in a way that manipulates the family and perpetuates the problem.

Emotional immaturity, another aspect of lack of identity, is a common problem among women who cannot cope in our society, and who turn to self-destructiveness. Immaturity shows in a child who consistently behaves like a younger child or in an adult who shows childish reactions. Everyone has some degree of 'immaturity' and will reveal it under some circumstances. What is important is the degree of control that we have over it, how we relate it to reality, how it shows in our relationships, and whether or not we use it creatively. Immaturity is not in itself self-destructive. Indeed it is probably essential for much creative work. Many immature adults are not at all self-destructive but if immaturity is retained, used or cherished as a way of life, or as a substitute for 'real me', it becomes self-destructive, particularly in a society such as ours.

According to her age the mature person is able to curb impulsiveness, delay satisfaction according to circumstances, make realistic appraisals and decisions and act on them, and be alone and independent when necessary. That person is also capable of living in what Fairbairn, a psychoanalyst who has made many distinguished contributions to this subject, has called 'mature dependency', with mutual support, trust and self-realization. Maturity includes the ability to foresee the likely effects of actions, to see the point of view of others and to take responsibility when this is appropriate. Moreover, emotional maturity does not stop with youth. It continues to develop into middle age and beyond. Together, appropriate maturity and a sense of 'real me' are the best defences against self-destructiveness.

An immature person lacks some, or all, of these qualities, and so is vulnerable. A child, if the family is sufficiently caring, is healthily protected from pressures and problems that are beyond its competence, while being allowed to exercise independence and judgment in matters suitable to its age and maturity. But an immature adult has no such protection, and when the environment fails to provide support, other methods have to be found to deal with the situation. These may be outwardly effective but, insofar as they prevent or destroy further personal development and fulfilment, they are self-destructive. The origins of self-destructiveness lie in demands with which the individual is unable to deal, often because they are unsuitable to that person's stage of maturity. These demands may come from outside, and so are demands from the environment, or they may come from within the mind itself.

Immature characteristics tend to persist together so that it is usually not possible to assess the separate effects of each. Nevertheless each tends to produce its own pattern of self-destructiveness.

Impulsiveness and the inability to wait for satisfaction are immature traits which lead easily to self-destructiveness. One young
woman would leave her desk at work whenever the impulse took
her. Without finding out whether it was convenient to others or
asking the permission of her boss, she would go shopping or visit her
boyfriend in his office on the other side of town. She frequently
telephoned her boyfriend on the office phone, thus annoying her
employers and her boyfriend. Finally she took to keeping a bottle of
whisky in her desk and taking nips whenever she felt like it. She had a
good job and was good at it, but eventually she was sacked. Soon
afterwards her boyfriend left her because he was unable to put up any
longer with her frequent impulsive demands.

Another woman was bored with her hard-working, successful
husband, whom she found 'dull'. Impulsively she set her sights on a
neighbour whom she was wont to waylay in the road outside his
home. Once she dramatically climbed down a ladder from her
bedroom to reach him. She was attractive and the neighbour suc-
cumbed. It became the scandal of the district. One night she went off
with the neighbour leaving her husband with their two small children. No sooner had she set up house with her lover than she began
to find him boring too. She quickly found another lover and travelled the world with him before deciding to return home as though
nothing had happened. By this time her husband had started divorce
proceedings and refused to take her back. The children were now
markedly disturbed. Since that time she has drifted from lover to
lover. She has matured somewhat with age and now regrets her
earlier impulsiveness.

Dependency is another characteristic of immaturity and can easily
become self-destructive. An example was Sue, a girl of twenty-two,
whose mother had always been subject to outbursts of rage, attacks
of depression and inconsistent behaviour towards her children. As
Sue grew up she did not experience the normal lessening of dependency on her mother. On the contrary, her dependent feelings
increased and she became one of those unfortunate people who are
forever seeking what they have never had and cannot find. In her case
this was a consistent, supportive mother's love. She was unable to go
away on holiday without her mother and was upset and miserable if
her mother left her even for a few days. In any situation outside
home, such as school, college or work, she immediately attached
herself to someone as a 'mother-substitute' and became dependent
on that person as long as she was there. At the age of twenty-one she
decided to make an effort to leave home. She took a job in a distant
town and lived in a hostel. Immediately she became infatuated with
Marie, an older woman at work. Sue manipulated her working day

as far as possible to be with Marie. This disrupted the work of the
department. No one there seems to have understood what was
happening, but the management was tolerant and efforts were made
to accommodate Sue. Every day after work, once she realized that
there was no further chance of seeing Marie that day, she returned to
the hostel and spent the evening writing poetry about her predicament and planning the next day to ensure the maximum contact with
Marie. She had no social life and made no effort to make one. She had
fantasies in which she would be ill and Marie would come and care
for her, wash her, and sit by her bedside talking or reading aloud, or
else she was locked up in a dungeon and Marie, against all odds,
would rescue her just before she died. One day at work, feeling that
she was receiving insufficient attention from her mother-figure, Sue
broke down and cried continuously until the head of the department
asked Marie to interrupt her own work and take Sue to the doctor. In
the doctor's surgery and in front of Marie, she 'confessed' how she
really felt about her. Marie was astonished, for she was herself an
attractive and not at all maternal young woman of twenty-eight.
Sue's employers continued to be accommodating for a few weeks
but later she was persuaded to hand in her resignation. With some
sense of relief, doubtless to her colleagues as well as herself, she
returned to her own mother.

Many dependent women choose the most available people in their
lives on whom to be dependent, often their husbands. Many select
husbands largely for fatherly qualities such as dependability and
knowledge of the world. The chosen man is often a person who is
flattered or made secure by feeling that a young and attractive person
is so dependent, and he encourages it. For a while, and occasionally
forever, such a marriage may seem firm and satisfying, though in
fact the woman, and often the man too, is making no progress
towards personal development. Such a woman may resist acquiring
experience and skill that might make her more independent. She
may refuse to learn to change a fuse, deal with the Gas Board or learn
to drive a car. Or she may insist on doing such things for her husband
in an attempt to keep him by her side as much as possible. She may
resent her husband's work and the demands it makes on his time and
on her opportunities for dependency. She may deliberately keep
herself as young as possible and act in a manner unsuited to her years.
A woman of this type often breaks down in middle life. She may
telephone her husband at his office many times a day or have hyster-
ics if he is not home at precisely the expected hour. She may make it
impossible for him to travel for his work. Even if the family budget
demands it she may be incapable of going out to work, and she may
rationalize this by saying that she 'believes' that a woman's place is in

the home. She may transfer some of her dependence on to her children and thus stifle their development. When things are going against her she may break down, become depressed or ill, or develop fears and phobias which necessitate her husband's frequent presence. Women with agoraphobia, an intense fear of public places such as streets and shops, are often dependent in this way. If the husband still finds his own security and satisfaction in caring for his dependent wife, he may devote himself to doing this regardless of the cost to the other areas of his life. But if he has increased in maturity and continued his own development, he may find the situation intolerable.

Self-centredness is another childish characteristic that often persists into adult life. Young children tend to think that they are the centre of the world and that everything and everybody can be influenced by them. Many normal adults have traces of this fantasy, but if it persists strongly it is self-destructive because it prevents a realistic appraisal of situations and interferes with the development of the capacity to see others as separate people. This has a disastrous effect on relationships. My impression is that this form of immaturity is commoner in men, in whom it is often encouraged by dependent or submissive women who then form bonds of mutual support and self-destructiveness. But self-centredness in other ways is commoner in women. These include the inability to appreciate that husbands and children have any life apart from them. Many self-centred women are unable to appreciate the importance of work to their husbands or the life their children lead with others of their age.

Competitiveness is a form of immaturity but it differs from those so far described in that it is not an inevitable accompaniment of immaturity. Many children grow up without being competitive. But competitiveness is sufficiently part of western culture for it to be induced in many children, by parents, teachers and other children. In some ways and in moderation it can have desirable consequences. But once established, it requires maturity to overcome it or to use it in a constructive way.

There are two main forms of competitiveness, and both tend to lead to self-destructiveness. One is found mainly in those of high intelligence or ability. They become accustomed to being better than everyone else, always top of the form. As they grow up the habit of being 'the best' becomes part of their personalities and they gear their lives to it. They avoid activities at which they do not shine, regardless of how enjoyable or useful those activities might be. If they meet a rival in their own field of excellence they react badly and may lie, cheat, or withdraw into illness in order to avoid the possibility of having to acknowledge that someone else is better. A feeling of lack of confidence that hampers normal life is sometimes a cover for this type of competitive self-destructiveness. Children who have the misfortune to grow up with this kind of 'superiority' have serious problems to overcome before they can lead adequate and progressive lives.

Sara, undoubtedly brilliant, was the cleverest pupil her small country school had ever had. Much praise and many prizes came her way. No other child in the school could beat her in any subject, and she also excelled at games and drama. The headmistress was ecstatic and wrote to Sara's mother about her daughter, using superlatives such as 'unprecedented achievement' and even 'genius'. Sara was fifteen when the Second World War broke out and another school was evacuated to hers. It soon became apparent that several of the visitors were as clever as Sara and that some were more advanced in formal subjects than she. Sara responded swiftly. Within two weeks of the new arrivals she had taken to her bed with a mysterious illness which neither the school doctor nor the specialists he called in, could diagnose. The illness lasted for three years, and by the time she had recovered Sara was behind with her education and insufficiently qualified for university. She took a job in a munitions factory and married a man much less intelligent than she. The marriage foundered but Sara gained a sense of self and insight into her problems. She was able to learn from her experiences. Today she is a successful author and also has the capacity to enjoy activities in which she is not outstanding.

The other type of competitiveness tends to arise in families where brothers and sisters compete with each other, usually for parents', or other siblings', affection and attention. We all know people who go through their whole lives competing in this way.

Many people who are unable to achieve or who are positively self-destructive are basically inadequate. By inadequate I mean unable to cope with the small problems of everyday life or with the larger decisions of life, or both. Some people are chronically indecisive or seem to make a mess of the simplest task. They tend to be dependent and insecure, fearful of the future, lacking confidence and a sense of 'real me', and anxious for someone else to take responsibility. They may drift into trouble, often finding that the only way they can express themselves is by being anti-social, or into illness because they feel they need help.

Julie felt she was inferior to her successful older sister, and that she could only win her parents' support by being helpless and pathetic. She was an intelligent girl but was unable to make the effort required for achievement. She tended to neglect her homework and, rather than face the consequences, played truant from school and feigned

illness. She became friendly with a crowd of young people and spent
much time in cafés and bars. She came before the juvenile court for
drunkenness and vandalism. Julie failed her O-levels through lack of
application. She moved into a squat with a boy but did nothing about
contraception. By the time she was seventeen she had had two
abortions, both organized by her parents, and had gone no further in
deciding what she wanted to do with her life.

Not all inadequate people come to disaster. Mary's family had a
successful betting shop in which she had a nominal job. In practice
she did little, but her salary was paid regularly and she was provided,
at the expense of the business, with a flat, a cleaner, and food. Mary
walked proudly, as though she played an important and honourable
part in the business. Only those who worked there knew the truth.

Some people use inadequacy as a way of life and as a means of
avoiding problems. More will be said of them later.

Submissiveness is part of the traditional woman's rôle but has
become one of the commonest forms of self-destructiveness is
women. The tendency to submit to whatever happens and to submerge one's own needs and development to the demands of others,
whether parents, husband, children, or all three, is the result of
dependency both emotional and economic, and also of training.
Submissiveness often comes out in women's work as secretaries,
personal assistants, domestics and in the so-called 'caring' professions. The equation of passivity with femininity and activity with
masculinity lies deep in our traditions and has been reinforced,
criticized, adapted and analysed by writers during this century. It is
ground that I do not intend to go over here.

Submissiveness today creates special problems for women. On
the one hand it is still widely believed that women should be submissive, though this is often disguised under euphemisms such as 'receptivity'. On the other hand there is a strong movement of protest, and
much of the present women's movement could be regarded as a fight
against submissiveness and an attempt to overcome it. But our
society still contains many submissive women and many who easily
become submissive. There are still many men who demand submissive wives and they are often the most conventionally attractive
men. Sexual submissiveness is still common and often takes the form
of the woman pretending to be satisfied when she is not. Yet the
world beckons and the number of submissive wives who believe
they are fulfilled is probably diminishing. A conflict is set up, often
the last thing a woman trained in submissiveness can tolerate. Thus
submissiveness, which is not always in itself self-destructive, turns
easily to self-destruction. It may lead to materialism or else to the
Doormat Syndrome, already described, in which the woman, who is

often able and talented and may have an independent career behind
her, marries a dominating, often protective, man and submits to him
totally, thereby encouraging his domineering and aggressive tendencies, often to their mutual unhappiness.

Beryl, herself penniless and untrained, married a rich man with an
ancient manor house but with very little intelligence, ability or
sensitivity. He was also greedy and lazy and expected Beryl to
submit at all times to his needs. Beryl ran the house, organized the
servants, ran his errands and made sure he was provided with three
elegantly cooked meals a day. If the slightest thing was wrong,
perhaps a dish was cold or there was dust on top of the door, he
would shout at her and vilify her. Sometimes he attacked her physically. Beryl accepted it all, aware of her lack of means and feeling
grateful to him for having taken her on. She also felt it to be the duty
of a wife to submit to whatever a husband chose to impose. The
years passed and the husband introduced his ancient and ailing
mother into the household and ordered Beryl to nurse and care for
her, which she did. The mother reacted with hostility and did all she
could to denigrate Beryl in her own and husband's eyes. The husband always believed his mother and regarded her endless complaints as a sign of Beryl's incompetence, for which he punished her
still further. The servants gradually left, unable to stand the atmosphere and the continual quarrelling. Beryl was left to run the large
house alone with a daily woman but she continued to nurse the old
lady and provide her husband, by now enormously fat, with his
three cooked meals a day. If she threatened to leave him, as she
occasionally did, he would bellow at her and assure her that she had
no rights in law and would find herself penniless. It did not occur to
her to consult a solicitor. Eventually Beryl died, worn out, of bron-
chitis and pneumonia. During the last months of her life she was
frequently cursed by her husband because she was too ill to attend to
his frequent demands.

Lisa was another doormat wife. Young and attractive, with two
small children, she followed wherever her husband led. Five times in
as many years she moved home and country at her husband's whim.
He had affairs with other women and boasted about them. He would
arrive at all hours, often with friends, and demand instant food. Lisa
kept her unhappiness to herself. Finally the family settled in England
and soon afterwards the husband's mother, recently widowed, followed them with her daughter and son-in-law. They all moved into
Lisa's house and Lisa had to sleep on the sofa to make room for them.
Her husband had a bed. She did all the cooking and cleaning and
coped with the children. Her husband gave her only a small allow-
ance for housekeeping but expected food of the highest quality for

himself and his relatives. He said he could not afford to give her more though he gave his mother £50 a week 'pocket money'. The children became disturbed and everyone blamed Lisa for being an inadequate mother. Eventually Lisa became seriously depressed. She was referred for treatment by her family doctor. She told me her story, which was confirmed unwittingly by her husband. I asked her, 'Why do you put up with this?' and she burst into tears and began to wonder why. Unlike many women in this kind of predicament, Lisa was a person who, given an ally and the right questions to think about, was able to help herself. She went to see a sympathetic solicitor to discover her legal position and found this was different from what her husband had told her. She challenged her husband and insisted on changes in the household as the condition of her staying. The husband, who was clearly more dependent on her than she had realized, gave way. He moved his relatives out and made efforts to improve his relationship with Lisa. The children were markedly happier and their teachers commented on it. Lisa started to read for a degree and now looks forward to increasing her independence and her satisfactions in life. Her husband, after much initial protest, has told her how much happier he now is and how glad he is that she made a stand. She has gained in self-confidence and swears that she will never again allow herself to slide into being a doormat.

Lisa was one of the lucky ones. In the end she was able to face her predicament, and to do something about it. Her depression was short-lived and related to her sense of helplessness and hopelessness. But many doormat women are unable to pull themselves up in this way.

Karen was a doormat for the whole family. She allowed full rein to her husband's controlling tendencies and she allowed her two teen-age sons to treat her as a slave. She cooked meals for them and their friends on demand, and never complained when they decided to go elsewhere at the last minute. When she asked her sixteen-year-old son to pick up his dirty clothes from the floor he shouted at her that it was beneath him to do such a thing as it was 'woman's work'. She drove her sons many miles a day, whenever the fancy took them, and if she was a few minutes late in fetching them, they swore at her. She also did all the dirty, boring work in the garden so that her husband could do what she called 'creative gardening' at the weekend. Eventually Karen developed a tremor so that she shook all day. She shook so much that she was unable to garden or cook or clean or drive the car. The tremor was diagnosed by different doctors but continued to get worse until Karen was severely disabled and unable to perform her duties as a doormat or as a sexual partner to her husband. Much later she admitted that she knew that the tremor was her form of 'shaking with rage' and that it was her escape from her impossible situation. With this insight the tremor improved, but it tends to come back whenever demands are made on her. She has been unable to find interests of her own or to develop herself further. She remains predominantly submissive though she is not such a doormat as she used to be.

In Karen we see many of the features that often accompany the Doormat Syndrome. There is depression, hopelessness, desire to escape and physical symptoms that are manipulative and used with hostility in retaliation. All these are important and common in self-destructive women.

I have dwelt at some length on the subject of submissive women because there are so many of them, and in the modern world they tend to fail.

A somewhat more positive, less destructive, type of submissiveness shows itself in endurance. The woman endures because she sees no satisfactory alternative, but when that alternative appears she takes it. She is less likely to react self-destructively though she often endures the intolerable at considerable cost to herself.

Margaret considered herself happily married until her husband developed a brain tumour, for which he had an operation. He seemed to make a good recovery but his character was changed. Previously he had been reasonable and gentle but was now unreasonable and violent, given to quick rages. He was often irritable, and no longer wanted to have anything to do with the children, though he had previously been an active and participating father. It seemed that Margaret could do nothing right and she felt that somehow her husband blamed her for his illness. Once, in a rage, he admitted to her that he did, but later he denied this. She went in fear of her life, for sometimes he even woke her in the night to attack her, and he was tall and powerful. Eventually the tumour recurred and he died. Margaret grieved but recovered. She feels the scars of what she went through but made a new life and eventually a new, and happy, marriage.

Compliance lies at the root of most self-destructiveness. It is a reaction to demands made by the environment which do not involve or stimulate an individual's spontaneity and sense of 'real me'. In healthy people compliance moulds the social self and is a valuable part of the person's make-up. But too much compliance forces the individual into a false existence, kills creativity and imagination and prevents the development of motivation and the sense of 'real me'. It leads to the growth of false relationships and impairs the use of symbols and the development of cultural life. Overcompliant people may appear to others, and even to themselves, to be like everyone else. They may have grown up identified with those close to them and living in these identifications. They may lead outwardly satisfying lives, being and doing what they feel they ought to be. But the sense of 'real me' is absent or buried or impossibly antisocial. They tend to become depressed and restless, to feel unsatisfied and unable to concentrate or to be involved in what they do, as though it had no real meaning. They may retreat into a fantasy world that has little connection with reality or they may search endlessly for more stimulation. Compliance, except in the healthy, social sense, is self-destructive.

Compliance has been the means by which many passive, submissive and dependent women have 'fitted in' through the ages and how many still do apparently fit in. Overcompliant people appear to be normal only as long as they remain supported by the environment to which they are adjusted. But since this adjustment depends on environmental support, if this is removed, even partially, they are thrown back on their own resources and then tend to flounder. Feelings of unreality, depression and futility supervene. The sense of purpose and involvement is lost and the falsity of the situation is revealed. It is because of this power of compliance to hold and support an individual within the environment that so many apparently well-adjusted people develop self-destructive traits, particularly at times of change or difficulty in their lives. One can sometimes see this occur in young children, for instance when starting or changing schools, or when their security is threatened, as when parents quarrel, separate or divorce. Adolescents, who have reached 'an age when it is necessary to enter a wider world and for the first time make personal decisions that will affect their future lives, often reveal their underlying compliance and lack of a sense of 'real me'. Adolescence is the time when most young people struggle to establish their true selves and most have to overcome some degree of compliance that they now find is hampering their progress. If they do not manage it they may become lifelong neurotics.

Some women break down in this way after marriage. An example was Jill, an intelligent, successful journalist, the daughter of two successful parents. She had been exceptionally independent at an early age and by the age of twenty-one she had saved enough money to pay a deposit on a mortgage and sufficient professional standing to be granted one. By her late twenties her name was a household word, and, living in her own house with a gay social life surrounded by clever and amusing friends, she seemed to be one of the most successful young people of her generation. Then she married, as she had always hoped to do. She liked her husband, and enjoyed her domesticity along with her work. Her sex life was also satisfactory.

But something in her rebelled against the state of marriage. She found she could not bear the idea of being married, and the more she thought about it the stronger grew her aversion. She became depressed, with strong urges to suicide accompanied by feelings of emptiness and of the futility of life. She no longer felt involved in her work but continued to do it mechanically. She gradually realized that marriage had somehow disrupted the shell of her life in which she had always lived. It made her aware of the emptiness and futility within. Eventually she separated from her husband, but the depression and the sense of futility persisted for a long time.

Childbirth can also disrupt a compliant life, and not always with the first child. Sometimes it seems to be associated with the birth itself, and abortion can have the same effect. Sometimes it may have more to do with the sex of the child or its resemblance to or association with one of the mother's parents. Sometimes being alone all day with a young baby brings on these feelings. Many women experience them when their children go to school, or leave home, or marry. Sometimes the underlying feelings of compliance are exposed by problems in marriage, especially if the husband becomes involved with another woman.

Jean had long regarded herself as stable and happily married and the successful mother of two daughters. When the girls were almost grown up her husband, who had always been supportive and reliable, began an affair with another woman. Jean went berserk. She destroyed all her husband's property that was left in the flat. She started to drink heavily, made repeated anonymous telephone calls to his girlfriend and would sit in her car outside the girlfriend's house for hours, abusing anyone who went in or out. At the same time she felt profoundly depressed and suffered from long attacks of weeping. Three times she took an overdose of drugs. She felt that her whole life was futile and that she must create as many scenes as possible to balance her inner emptiness. In fact, her husband had no real desire to break up the marriage, but as a result of Jean's behaviour he decided to leave and end the marriage as soon as he could. Their daughters went with him. Jean was left alone with her depression and her emptiness, having destroyed everything that was precious and supportive to her.

Few people are so positive and in touch with their true selves as not to develop some self-destructive traits when faced with a crisis or stress, though they do not usually act as destructively as Jean. Indeed, under some circumstances, it can be self-destructive not to feel, for a limited period, depressed or unreal or hopeless or uncreative. Some people suppress such feelings under circumstances when it would be healthier to acknowledge them. This is another form of compliance and of self-destructiveness.

Living vicariously is allied to submissiveness and is a form of self-destructiveness to which women are particularly prone. A woman who works in the home all day or who has a job that does not satisfy her can easily slip into a state of mind in which her only satisfactions come from serving her husband and children or her boss and from being involved in their lives rather than in her own. Such a woman often pays so little attention to herself that she becomes an empty shell, with no life of her own. When the children grow up or the husband grows away, she is left with the emptiness and is conscious only of the void, unable to make progress in her life. She may sink into depression or hopelessness, take to drink or hypochondriasis, or indulge in emotional blackmail, manipulating husband and children to keep them close to her and fill her empty life, organizing this as the price of her health and equilibrium.

Judy and her husband brought up their two sons and a daughter in the country, far from schools and public transport. This meant that for twenty years Judy spent much of her time driving to and from the town, the various schools attended by her children, and their various social engagements. She was ambitious for them and wanted them to be accomplished. Riding, skating, tennis, dancing and music lessons greatly increased the time she spent driving. In addition they had a pony and other pets which she mostly looked after herself, as well as cleaning, housekeeping and cooking delicious meals for them all to enjoy. She had no friends and no interests of her own. When the elder son bought a motor cycle and so achieved some independence, she became depressed. When her daughter wanted to leave home to work in London she raised every possible objection. By the time all the children had left home she was a difficult and unhappy woman. She took to drink and became severely alcoholic. Eventually she agreed to go away for treatment, but it was impossible to treat her because her one idea was to get her children home again. She tried by every possible means to persuade her daughter to come home and look after her. She tried to destroy all her children's friendships and marriages. Whenever she was thwarted in her desires she had another bout of heavy drinking, combined with further pleas to her children to come home to her.

Boredom is a common manifestation of compliance and lack of a sense of 'real me'. Some women who tend to suffer from it avoid it by making sure they are always active. Boredom is self-destructive because it militates against personal involvement and personal development. People who have a strong sense of themselves are seldom bored because they find the world so full of interest that even if they are obliged to perform tasks that are in themselves boring they make something out of these tasks for themselves and are thereby enriched. Boredom often goes with lack of confidence, superficiality, narcissism, materialism and depression.

Those who boast that they never have a spare minute are often staving off boredom and depression that go with emptiness and compliancy. Such women often take pride in the beautifully-run lives, take on extra jobs or sit on innumerable committees and are always darting hither and thither. They tend to try to escape from themselves and from their lack of a sense of themselves.

Superficiality is often associated with either boredom or hyperactivity. It develops naturally with these because both prevent development and depth. Superficiality itself can also be a defence against awareness of emptiness and compliancy. Only concerning oneself with trivial matters can be a means of receiving stimulation from the environment without the work and pain involved in benefiting from it.

One of the many ways by which self-destructive people maintain adjustment and equilibrium is by playing rôles and attempting to conform to stereotypes. The perfect wife, the good mother, the welcoming hostess, the career woman, the committee woman and the voluntary worker are all common rôles.

If most of life is reduced to rôle-playing, relationships are effectively controlled within the boundaries imposed by these and so are made safe. Self-destructive people are often made anxious by unstructured relationships, which demand spontaneity, genuineness and creativity. If one functions only as Bill's wife, Little Willy's mother, or the chairperson at the meeting, none of these qualities is demanded. I am not implying that these qualities are never used in these rôles or that all good wives, mothers, committee members and so on are of this type, only that some are.

'The one thing you can say about my wife is that she's a perfect wife and mother,' said the father of a severely depressed adolescent girl. But the story told by the girl, which was confirmed inadvertently by both parents, was different. After her marriage at the age of 34, the mother had given up her previous rôle of 'perfect doctor' to devote herself totally to her husband and later her children. Like Judy, who lived vicariously through her family, this lady spent eighteen years devoting herself entirely to their needs. She managed to instil into her children the standards she expected them to live up to, and these were the highest. Extreme cleanliness and godliness were the order of the day, together with high academic achievement, associating only with 'suitable' friends and using all available time profitably. There was no opportunity in this régime for spontaneous activity, personal variance or creative activity. Pop music and trendy clothes were out of the question and writing poetry was strongly discouraged. School prizes and the praise of teachers often came the children's way but finding things out for themselves and making their own mistakes had never been part of their lives. Now this girl, at the age of seventeen, was not sure what she wanted to do. She wanted to please her mother and get good A-levels, but it all seemed so pointless. If she went to university she would have to leave home and face that terrifying freedom. And for what? She did not know. Sometimes she found herself bad-tempered and unhelpful to her mother and she had no idea why. She felt confused and guilty.

Rôle-playing does not always aim at the superlative. Sometimes women play the rôles of hopeless housewife, forgetful mother, scatty women-trying-to-run-both-home-and-a-job. The importance of rôle-playing is that it is not totally genuine. To some extent everyone has to play rôles. But when this is excessive it is usually because the rôle is used as a substitute for the real self and is a defence against developing that self and against being spontaneous and imaginative.

Professional rôle-playing, such as the acting profession, can be an expression of the true self and those who use their profession in this way are mostly the best. Others use it as a substitute. Some professional actors and actresses, particularly the less successful ones, choose their profession so that rôles can fill their emptiness. They suffer from emptiness whenever they cannot compensate in this way.

Professional rôle-playing as a substitute for living is by no means confined to the acting profession. There are many others who only survive as people through the part they play at work. For instance, being a doctor, lawyer or shopkeeper provides a safe, structured situation within which it is possible to function in a controlled way, free from the dangers of spontaneity. One of the hazards of professional involvement and success is the tendency to bury the true self and to become increasingly an empty person playing a known part. The French have a phrase for it, *déformation professionelle*. It may be that men suffer from this form of self-destructiveness even more than women.

Many people who are unsure of themselves seek attention from others, and attention-seeking is a form of reassurance. The habit usually begins in childhood and, while most people grow out of it, many do not. Many revert to this type of behaviour when life is difficult. Attention-seeking can become a way of life and the strongest means by which a person relates to the outside world. It can take many forms in adults, including exaggerated appearance and dress, dramatic gestures and behaviour, physical illness and

symptoms, and high achievement. Attention-seeking can be a form
of compliance or a means of coping with a difficult environment. It
can also be a form of control or attempted control. Destructive
threats of this type are probably even more common than destructive actions. Women who are trying to manipulate situations to
attract attention to themselves often threaten that they will leave
home, leave the children or commit suicide.

Attention-seeking behaviour is often a statement of personal need,
but the real need is not for the attention but for the satisfaction and
peace of mind that goes with the feeling of 'real me'. Thus it is often a
kind of search for the true self. But in practice it masks the true self
and makes this even less accessible. In this way it is self-destructive.

Women whose self-respect is low, who are usually far removed
from their own true selves, are often actively destructive when they
seek attention and they may damage either themselves or others.
Some women get drunk when they feel particularly in need of
attention. One woman jumped from a second-floor hospital win-
dow. She landed neatly, doubtless with premeditation, in a flower
bed, but she broke her an ankle and spent the next seven years suing
the hospital for failing to take adequate precautions. Another
woman, whenever she felt that her husband or children were paying
insufficient attention to her, would set fire to the house. She did this
nine times and not only destroyed her family's possessions but
caused her husband endless anxiety and trouble, not least with the
insurance company, until in the end he divorced her, which was not
at all what she had intended.

Narcissism is a character trait that tends to be self-destructive.
Narcissus fell in love with his own image and many self-destructive
people do the same. Like attention-seeking, which often co-exists
with it, narcissism takes many forms. A common type, and perhaps
the most characteristic and obvious, was Diana, lovingly preserved
and in her fifties. In her youth she had been a successful fashion
model. Her whole life seemed to revolve around assuring herself that
she was still young and beautiful. She arrived in hospital after a
suicidal gesture carrying a large beauty case full of lotions, creams
and make-up. She was heavily sedated as part of her treatment but
despite this she managed to drag the beauty case into the bed and
spent hours each day making up her face and removing all the
make-up carefully each night. She made desperate attempts to attract
the attention of every man who appeared. When allowed up she
walked around in a transparent nightdress and bare feet, talked
endlessly to any man available, and often asked him to admire her
tiny feet. She was gushingly friendly to anyone who made an admir-
ing remark and tended to be hostile to anyone who did not. Her bed

was surrounded by photographs of herself when young and a large scrap book of old press cuttings lay at the ready beside her.

Less obviously but equally narcissistic was Virginia. She too was a hospital patient. She was naturally pretty but did little about her appearance. Her self-loving compulsion was to win the heart of every man who came her way and, if possible, to seduce him. Her success in this caused trouble with the wives of male patients and with the nursing staff. She was quietly discharged after being found at 4 a.m. in bed with a young alcoholic.

Penelope was narcissistic, not so much about her looks which were ordinary, but about her brains and her wit. These were not inconsiderable but her own infatuation with them led her to display them inappropriately and in manner which usually left herself as the sole admirer. Her caustic, although often perceptive, comments to and about other people caused embarrassment and many people feared and disliked her, often while admitting that she was amusing company. She was actually a lonely, insecure person, desperately anxious for love and unable to understand why her relationships always broke up. In her one could see how narcissism is often an attempt to get stimulation from the world with which to fill the void within.

A different form of narcissism leads to preoccupation with the functioning of the self, usually bodily but sometimes psychologically. If one is totally involved in the way one's body or mind functions it will not be long before one is conscious of variations and small irregularities. If, in answer to the question 'How are you?' one answers in detail or (as in the case of a bowel fanatic) 'I haven't managed to go yet today,' then one is a bore and incompetent in normal social relationships. If one thinks constantly about one's heart one becomes conscious of its beating and of its occasional irregularity. By this process any part of the body can be induced to produce symptoms, and at the same time one loses connection with the outside world and this is self-destructive. The process is unconscious, and the origin of much self-medication, particularly with sleeping pills, slimming pills and laxatives.

Psychological narcissism of this type is not uncommon in a society which abounds in psychoanalysis and its derivatives, and hundreds of different forms of self-help groups and books on popular psychology. It is not unusual for people nowadays to monitor every thought and feeling that comes to them and then interpret these according to whatever theoretical structure they have attached to their beliefs and fantasies. Sometimes psychiatric patients of the 'permanent' kind make remarks such as 'I feel quite well and happy today but I can't work out why.'

Our society is one in which women pay much attention to making themselves attractive to others. This of course is not usually self-destructive. But there are several forms of attractiveness and some of them can be self-destructive.

Of the different types of attractiveness first, and usually the most atractive to most people, is what we might call natural attractiveness. Some people seem to be born with face, figure, personality, or a combination of these, that appeals to others without artificial aid. Second, and more common, is the type of attractiveness whose aim is to enhance the self and communicate it to others. This usually goes with the aim of concealing blemishes or less attractive features. Neither of these types of attractiveness is self-destructive. In fact we could say that failure to seek this form of attractiveness is, or can be, in itself a form of self-destructiveness. A woman who is badly dressed or wears no make-up when she could look much better with it, may be expressing something that is real to her but she is also destroying some of her potential.

There are however forms of attractiveness, or attempts at attractiveness, which aim to conceal the self, substitute for the self or hide its absence. The desired attractiveness is then a mask and it is interesting that such a woman often wears make-up as a mask rather than as an enhancement of her natural looks. This can be quite striking. She is also likely to feel uncomfortably naked or exposed if caught without her mask. Such women sometimes talk about 'putting on my face' in the morning. Women to whom attractiveness is a concealment or substitute for self are often painfully self-conscious. For instance, one young woman would not go out because a particular shade of lipstick was no longer available. She believed that it was the only one that suited her and she could not face the world without it. Another refused to see any of her friends because she had gained 3 lbs in weight and she felt that as a result no one would like her or want to be with her any more.

An exaggerated search for attractiveness can also be an attention-seeking device, either revealing the need to be loved or pandered to or else for purposes of control. Some women doll themselves up excessively because they find that this gives them power over men, whom they may wish to hurt or humiliate. Some women make themselves attractive in this way not in order to attract their husbands or boyfriends but in order to attract others and so arouse jealousy. This is destructive of relationships and so is ultimately self-destructive.

Women, like men, are often self-destructive in their choice of whom they find attractive. Just as the diffident man who is unsure of himself often eschews the gentle, caring girl who could help him with his difficulties and is attracted to confident, experienced women, attractive to many men, highly critical, and likely to snub or 'castrate' him, so women who are unsure of themselves or miserable in the life they lead often fall for urbane sophisticated men, often of a narcissistic type. Such a man knows how to flatter and cajole and the woman, desperate for love and sympathy, becomes wholly devoted and virtually his slave. To him she is another conquest, someone else to boost his self-admiration. But to her he is her whole life.

Frances, in her middle thirties and with teenage children, was totally dependent financially on her husband who treated her as something subhuman. He expected his meals to be waiting, yet did not tell her whether or when he was coming home. He cursed her in front of the children, and frequently shouted at her and abused her. He demanded sex frequently, yet refused all physical contact except the purely genital. He would leave home without warning for several days at a time and shout at her if she was upset. He showed no consideration or affection. It was not surprising that she was overwhelmed when another man began to court her, and fell deeply in love. This man had a devoted wife and, Frances later learned, also several mistresses and many girlfriends. Even when she knew this he still managed to make her feel that she was the one and only person for whom he really cared. She was prepared to follow him to the ends of the earth and they made plans to elope together. It is unlikely that the man was ever serious. He broke appointments with her, he frequently failed to telephone as promised and she knew that he went out with other women. But Frances was so desperate that she was prepared to put up with anything to keep his attention. She worshipped him for four years until she finally realized, in her heart as well as her head, that he was feeding off her devotion and giving almost nothing back. Eventually she broke off the association and took steps to deal with her problems in more constructive ways than waiting for a telephone which hardly ever rang.

Some women are self-destructive as a form of compensation for what they feel they need or miss or else as an escape from the burdens and anxieties of their lives. It is often not possible to separate these. The excessive use of food or drink is often indicative of both these kinds of self-destructiveness. So is materialism. Money is often both sought and spent as a form of compensation or escape, and it seems to be true that many men seek compensation or escape by making more money than they need, and many women with the same urges go out on spending sprees, because buying something gives temporary relief from depression. This difference between the sexes is probably due to the fact that women on the whole have more time than men. Many people are aware that if they are not engaged in actively making money they have a tendency to go out and spend it.

Basic feelings of insecurity are important in self-destructiveness. Even those who are apparently the most secure can have their lives shattered at any moment and many of those who appear to have little or no security do not worry about it. No one is really secure and everyone knows the feeling of insecurity. But to be dominated by a sense of insecurity in ordinary life, or to feel that it is of vital importance to achieve security, is self-destructive. It is not possible to be secure. Thus a woman of twenty-nine, conscious of the years slipping by, was unable to make up her mind to marry a man who had courted her for six years. 'The problem is,' she explained, 'that I feel I must be absolutely sure that the marriage will work out well. Unless I *know* that it will be all right, I daren't take the plunge.' When reminded of the song *Che sera, sera,* 'Whatever will be will be, The Future's not ours to see', she replied, 'That's not my style. I couldn't live like that', and was unable to see the unreality of her feelings.

Feelings of insecurity without gross deprivation are feelings of anxiety, and the inability to tolerate anxiety lies at the root of much self-destructiveness. Basic pessimism can generate anxiety, but basic optimism prevents it from developing even in the most inauspicious circumstances.

In ordinary life, when people complain of or admit to feelings of insecurity they are usually suffering from anxiety and this usually means that they are trying to live and base themselves in the shell of their personalities and avoiding the core. They are likely to have little sense of 'real me'. They may be searching for themselves, going through some kind of identity crisis, they may be avoiding themselves or they may be trying to manipulate the environment.

Lack of confidence is a common form of insecurity in women and a common cause for complaint. Women often give it as the reason why they are unable to do something that they otherwise would like to do, even when it is something that they are well qualified to do. Lack of confidence is a form of anxiety and often an escape from anxiety. By not having the confidence to do something one avoids the anxiety and effort involved in doing it, and also the personal development that would ensue. These motives are nearly always unconscious but this does not reduce their self-destructiveness.

Women usually notice lack of confidence at times of change in their lives and most commonly, in my experience, in middle life. When they have achieved their ambitions or their children become independent and they need to find something else to occupy themselves they are often assailed by lack of confidence. The idea of entering or returning to the working world or making a change gives rise to intolerable anxieties and they feel they 'haven't the confidence' to do it. Sometimes the lack of confidence extends to minor household duties and is then likely to be an unconscious attempt to manipulate the family. One woman, when her children became too old to require her constant and conscientious attention lost all her self-confidence and was incapable of even boiling an egg, let alone cook complicated meals and run the household as she had for the previous twenty years. Her husband and children were forced to take over many of her duties, which meant that she kept them by her. She 'lacked the confidence' even to remain alone in the house, so the family tried to organize their lives so that someone was always with her.

But lack of confidence, like some other self-destructive traits, is sometimes a symptom of a depressive illness and as the depression lifts, so confidence returns. But in the absence of a true depression, and often in its presence too, lack of confidence usually means a lack of 'real me' and often a determination not to progress. Lack of confidence is often related to perfectionism and the idea that if one cannot do something superlatively well, or even if there is any danger that one might not do it to perfection, it is safer to avoid it. It is often related to competitiveness and the feeling that one must be 'top'. In this instance, if there is any possibility that someone else will be better, one drops out.

Trying to please others is part of a woman's traditional rôle. At best it is an expression of her true self, in which case she has plenty of reserves and resources of her own and is capable of developing them and using them. But sometimes it is merely a reflection of her lack of sense of self and a cover-up for her own immaturity and emptiness. Often such a woman found in early childhood that the only comfortable way to live was by pleasing others and to this compliant end she suppressed all personal drives and progress.

Women who relate to others only by trying to please them can, of course, be extremely pleasant and, as long as the pleasing is not irritatingly sycophantic, they may be well-liked. As a child such a girl is often 'mother's little girl' or 'teacher's pet', and she may develop remarkable skill in attending to the wants of others. Later she tends to choose boyfriends and husband who like to be pleased and pandered to and they may exploit her pleasing self-destructiveness. She learns no other way of life. She sets out to please her in-laws, her children, her friends and her employers. They may well find her delightful and indispensable, but she pays a price for this particular form of compliance. The price is her self, which tends to be forgotten or lost. One day she may suddenly realize this and break out of her self-imposed straitjacket. She may go through some form of identity crisis, or suffer a depression, or rebel in one way or another, perhaps losing all confidence or developing fears and phobias or becoming physically ill. Or she may turn the tables subtly on those she is accustomed to pleasing, harden her personality, and become a rebel or a martyr.

Jealousy, certainly a self-destructive emotion, encourages lack of self-respect because it often leads to behaviour incompatible with self-respect. Jealousy involves three people in a situation in which two of them compete either in fact or in imagination, for the attention of a third. Not surprisingly it frequently occurs in its more extreme forms in women who are attached to rather narcissistic, self-loving men, who like to show attention to others and enjoy arousing jealousy in those who care for them. A woman who finds it necessary to check on every moment in her husband's day may well discover that he lunches with another woman, and her perpetual checking may encourage him to do so and to feel pride in thus outwitting her. This kind of behaviour is often self-destructive on both sides. Some men are totally trustworthy and everyone but their wives can see this. But this very quality often attracts women whose insecurity makes them liable to be jealous. One man who had never been unfaithful to his wife received an innocuous Christmas card from a typist in his office whom he scarcely knew. His wife saw the card and for the next three years scarcely a day passed without her mentioning it, raving angrily about it or questioning him about it. She would sniff his suit when he arrived home in the evening to find out if it smelled of scent. He became afraid to sit next to a woman on the train home in case the smell of her scent passed to his clothes.

Envy, according to the Oxford English Dictionary, is 'the feeling of mortification and ill-will occasioned by the contemplation of superior advantages possessed by another.' It is a self-destructive feeling related to suppressed anger and closely associated with feelings about oneself. It occurs largely in people whose self-respect is low and who lack a sense of 'real me'. Such people often appear to be confident and even cocky but their envy is a false, ultimately self-destructive cover for their emptiness. People who have a strong sense of 'real me' sometimes feel envy in another sense, i.e. 'a longing for the advantages enjoyed by another person' (O.E.D.) and this may be stimulus towards achievement and self-realization.

Unlike jealousy, which essentially involves three people, envy involves only two. It can often be seen not so much as an emotion felt by one person towards another but as part, sometimes a dominant part, of a person's relationship to the environment. The person with a 'chip on the shoulder' tends to reveal it in many different situations.

Boundary-seeking is an appropriate name for a particular form of self-destructive behaviour that is common in young people and also occurs in adults. The person who indulges in this form of behaviour seems to have an irresistible urge to test relationships by seeing just how far he or she can go before the relationship changes. In a child it often goes with a sense of insecurity about whether the parents really love him and also with a need to find out whether there are limits to this love, and in adult life this is extended to other relationships. To some extent boundary-seeking is part of normal growing up and normal adolescent rebellion but it can be extreme.

Philippa's father was a doctor and a highly respected member of the community in a small country town. He was a practical outdoor man who enjoyed sharing activities with his children and as long as they were outgoing and easy-going he got along well with them. But at the age of twelve Philippa changed. She lost interest in her pony and in sailing and became dreamy and withdrawn. Her mother, a schoolteacher, comforted the father in the loss of his daughter from the activities he so much loved and assured him that Philippa was going through a 'normal' phase. But soon both parents became alarmed. Philippa made friends with some older boys and girls, many of whom, according to her parents, were 'the worst elements in the town' and some of whom had police records. Philippa began to drink heavily and obtained illegal drugs. Her behaviour changed. She became violent and difficult, apparently unable to tolerate the slightest frustration. If asked to clean her room or help with the washing-up she would fly into a temper and smash the crockery. She refused to stay at home in the evenings and sometimes stayed out all night with her friends or slept in their cars. She truanted from school whenever she felt like it. Several times she was brought back by the police and by the time she was sixteen she had several convictions for drunkenness, vandalism and being in possession of cannabis and 'speed'. At one point she was taken into the care of the local authority and spent a month in a home, but was no better after this chastening experience. She seemed to derive pleasure in humiliating her parents in public and much enjoyed their discomfort when she made headlines in the local paper. Her parents tried to understand her and believed that much of her behaviour was due to the influence of her friends and of the drugs she sought so relentlessly. The more they tried to understand and not to condemn, the worse Philippa's behaviour became. Her parents protested but found it impossible to impose limits or sanctions, fearing that she would leave home altogether and not only be lost to them but also go completely to the bad. She brought boys back to the house and slept with them there. She grew a cannabis plant in her room and dared her parents to take it from her. She became pregnant and her father arranged an abortion. Several times she provoked her father, usually a gentle man, into hitting her. He became alarmed at his own aggressive feelings but was still unable to control her or improve his relationship with her. But **Philippa** gradually matured. She is now nineteen and is studying design at a local college. Her relationship with her parents is wary. She continues to take drugs and occasionally gets drunk. There are still episodes at home that cause her parents to despair. But she has been out of serious trouble for two years and she attends her classes with reasonable diligence. She now understands that she has an urge to test her parents' love, and sometimes, she admits, the desire to 'find the boundaries' overwhelms her.

At the age of eighteen Betty married a steady, reliable man fifteen years older than she. At first all went well and they had two children. By the time Betty was twenty-five they were both at school and Betty began to think of all that she had missed by marrying so young. She felt that she had wasted her youth. She neglected the house so much that her husband felt obliged to do the housework. She made overtures to other men and had several affairs. When her husband accepted this behaviour, albeit reluctantly, she taunted him with tales of her lovers' sexual prowess. She would 'forget' to buy food or to fetch the children from school. She became abusive to her husband and would throw plates and furniture at him. She would disappear for days at a time, leaving him to cope with the children as best he could. Her husband tried to be as patient and understanding as he could. He endured her peccadillos, her temper, her erratic behaviour. He tried to provide the children with love and stability. But finally his endurance came to an end and he started divorce proceedings. Immediately Betty changed and took steps to repair the marriage. Having found the limits to which she could push him she decided to be more positive about her marriage relationship. Two years later the family seemed stable and happy.

Most people seem to have a sense, rather than knowledge, of what the boundaries are in their relationships and if they care about the relationship they stay well within them. Most people also have a sense of how far they are prepared to allow another person to go. If they make a point of defining these boundaries they are likely to be rigid, controlling and unimaginative. But when the boundary is reached, they know immediately and act accordingly. Those who lack a sense of boundary in a close relationship are likely unconsciously to provoke the kind of behaviour described in these two cases, and thus inadvertently encourage the self-destructiveness.

Success or failure in women depends on specific qualities of personality interacting with the environment. For women in most societies, both in the past and in the present, the most successful personality, at least in the sense of absence of self-destructiveness, has been one that is submissive, accepting, unquestioning and unenlightened. It has included the ability to submerge the self into traditional activity, a capacity for endurance, including the capacity to endure boredom, either boredom due to the nature of necessary tasks or the boredom due to having too little to do. Acceptance of traditional values and the ability to transmit them has been very important, and with this usually goes the lack of a sense of conflict and the ability to suppress what is not acceptable, as one sees in the traditional three monkeys who hear, see and speak no evil. To do all this successfully a high level of personal development is not only unnecessary but tends to be a disadvantage. It is certain that many women living such a life have suppressed a great deal of unhappiness but, because they are supported by the society in which they live, it does not often appear in the form of overt self-destructiveness. It is true that many Victorian maidens languished on couches and suffered from a strange disease called *chlorosis,* and many Muslim women today suffer from multiple physical symptons or outbursts of hysteria, but on the whole they were not and are not aware of the possibility of choice, unless they stumbled on it by chance, like Nora in Ibsen's *The Doll's House.* Nor were they or are they as self-destructive as modern women in the western world today. Anna Karenina is a magnificent study of a self-destructive woman in a traditional society, but the other women in Tolstoy's novel conform to expected patterns.

The personality that survives and is successful in modern western society is very different. As we have seen, she needs a high degree of personal development, a strong sense of self, and a strong sense of her own worth. She needs the ability to adapt to rapid social change while retaining whatever strength she derives from her roots. This involves the ability to tolerate conflict, to see the next stage, to foresee possible consequences and adapt to them and, most important, the capacity to tolerate anxiety. Because of the conflicts in the various rôles she has to play, she needs to be able both to control and not to control, and to please without feeling a necessity to please. She needs to be able to support herself both emotionally and financially, even if she does not always have to do this. She needs to be questioning, enlightened, and able to change her views. Essential too is the capacity to choose and to choose correctly, whether it be partner, work or motherhood. In addition she has to cope with the demands of society, whether or not she herself agrees with them. The media exhort her to be sexually attractive and slim, to possess all traditional virtues, and to be talented, yet not to appear to be too intelligent. For most people these are impossible combinations.

In addition, many other qualities make for individual variation in any society. These include some already discussed, such as self-centredness, dependency, jealousy, and others such as the capacity to care for others, charm, greed, power-seeking and a sense of humour. Some women would be self-destructive in any society, for example, Lady Caroline Lamb. They do not usually reach the history books, and she only did because she was Byron's mistress and the wife of a man who was to become Prime Minister.

Chapter Five

Women Against Life

Certain types of women, and women with certain problems, are particularly liable to develop self-destructive tendencies. Especially liable are those who suffer from excessive anxiety or who have a poor capacity for dealing with anxiety.

Anxiety is a feeling of apprehension, usually unpleasant, which may or may not be related to an obvious cause, but which always contains elements of uncertainty. Everyone experiences it sometimes, for instance, before an important event such as getting married or taking an examination or, in family situations, perhaps when a child is missing or a loved one seriously ill, or when there is external danger, such as an impending car or plane crash. In each case one is not sure what is going to happen and the uncertainty increases the fear.

Although anxiety is often discussed as if it is something always to be avoided or to be treated with drugs, it is not inherently self-destructive. Anxiety is often an inevitable and desirable reaction and sometimes its absence rather than its presence is self-destructive. Not to feel anxious at certain times can have serious, even catastrophic consequences, for anxiety is often the stimulus to desirable action. For instance, most people who have to perform or speak in public feel some anxiety before an appearance and absence of anxiety on such an occasion can lead to a flat performance. Or if one's child is unhappy at school absence of anxiety may mean that one fails to do anything about it.

But most people at some time in their lives, and some people for most of their lives, experience irrational anxiety and this tends to be self-destructive. One kind of irrational anxiety is an excessive reaction to an outside event. One may be so anxious about getting married that one cancels the wedding, even though one has previously made a rational decision that this is what one wants. Anxiety about sex may lead to impotence or frigidity. One may be so anxious about an examination that one fails it, even though one knows the syllabus. One may be so anxious about one's child that one never lets him out of one's sight and as a result his development may be distorted, which will have repercussions on the whole family and so be destructive to oneself as well.

Another type of irrational anxiety seems to appear without cause. It comes from within and one does not understand what it is about. People often wake up in the night or early morning with anxiety welling up inside them.

Yet another type of anxiety fixes itself on to specific objects or situations even when they are known to be harmless. It may be set off by cats or spiders or ambulances, or it may be associated with enclosed spaces (claustrophobia) or public places (agoraphobia). These specific fears and phobias will be dealt with later.

Sometimes anxiety seems to build itself into the personality and is evident in everything about the person. Such a person may feel chronically anxious or be endlessly involved with problems, many of which may even not have arisen. A person who is constantly worrying about problems rather than their solutions is usually a chronically anxious person. Such anxiety is self-destructive for it patently destroys personal life, development and fulfilment.

Learning to tolerate anxiety and to deal with it is an important part of growing up. A child learns to tolerate it largely through contact with his parents and with others who have more mature ways of dealing with it. Failure in this can lead to a lifetime of self-destructiveness. Anxiety and the inability to deal with it in constructive and productive ways underlies many other forms of self-destructiveness.

Neurotic women of all types tend to be self-destructive. Because the word is used as a noun, it is widely believed that a neurosis is a *thing,* something inside the mind that causes trouble and can be sought, identified and rooted out or dispelled. In fact, neurosis is more a consistent way of feeling and behaving that is inappropriate to circumstances. The inappropriate feelings and ways of behaving are based on anxiety, which may be conscious or unconscious. The methods chosen, albeit unconsciously, to deal with this anxiety, tend to be aberrant and self-destructive. There are different types of neurosis and they are not all clearly defined. Hysteria is sometimes referred to as a neurosis, and so are fears and phobias. The chronically anxious and over-reactive person is likely to be labelled a 'neurotic personality'.

One of the most clearly defined forms of neurosis is obsessional neurosis. In this condition the sufferer is assailed by thoughts, desires and impulses, often of an aggressive or sexual nature, which seem to come 'out of the blue', and to be opposed to the person's normal thoughts. These thoughts and desires often cause much distress and are accompanied by an excessive preoccupation with detail, constant checking and rechecking, and compulsions to carry out certain actions, such as frequent washing, and other repetitive rituals.

A virgin spinster aged fifty-eight became preoccupied with the idea of men's genitals inside their trousers. Every time she saw a man she could not stop herself looking between his legs. If she saw any evidence of a bulge, the same series of words invariably came into her mind: 'Shit cock fuck cunt cock shit' and these were repeated several times. She resisted the desire to shout them out but always feared that she might do so. After such an episode she felt impelled to seek the nearest cloakroom and wash her hands twenty-five times. Always twenty-five. Since she worked in an estate agent's office, this happened many times a day and it became impossible for her to get through her work or to have any social life. For a while she stayed at home, imprisoned by her neurosis and increasingly involved in compulsive rituals. From cases like this it is not difficult to see why neurosis is self-destructive.

Depression also plays an important part in self-destructiveness. The word depression is used to describe a mood, a permanent state of mind or an episodic condition that is part of a personality or an illness. Most people experience it at some time. Characteristically, a feeling of sadness or despair follows the loss or abandonment of some loved person, ambition or project. This is mourning, a state that is akin to depression and often merges with it.

Mourning after a painful loss is not self-destructive. In such circumstances failure to mourn is more likely to have self-destructive consequences. Similarly, temporary depression after an illness, particularly an infectious illness, can be part of convalescence, the restoration to full health. If sadness and grief are prolonged beyond what seems reasonable it may be turning into a depressive illness. This is not usually any more self-destructive that any other illness. It takes time to recover, and, like any other illness, can usually be cured. It temporarily suspends progress in life rather than injures it. Similarly I would not classify as self-destructive those severe depressions that come 'out of the blue', last for weeks or months, and are not alleviated by changes in the environment. They are self-destructive in the sense that, if untreated, they may lead to suicide but, provided this does not happen, they do not necessarily or permanently affect progress and fulfilment any more than any other illness, and the patient who recovers is usually able to pick up the threads of life again.

Self-destructive depression is the kind that comes frequently after small disappointments and failures, and sometimes for no apparent reason, does not usually last more than a few hours or days, and is alleviated, at least temporarily, by changes in the environment. Such depressions are usually part of a neurotic and self-destructive personality and reveal someone who is either searching for true identity or else has given up the struggle and is living unhappily with her own emptiness.

Much self-destructive behaviour can be seen as a form of escape. The escape is from emptiness of personality and lack of a sense of 'real me', or from the conflicts of ordinary life. All conflicts tend to arouse anxiety but people with a strong sense of self are usually equipped to deal with it. People whose sense of self is deficient tend to experience intolerable anxiety when faced with conflict and so, understandably, they are more likely to try to escape from it. A desire for escape can therefore be seen in many forms of self-destructive behaviour. Immature or submissive behaviour can be an escape from the conflicts of being adult and is most commonly and most normally seen in adolescence, when a sense of identity is often found to be necessary but has not yet fully developed. Compliant behaviour and attention-seeking behaviour are also often increased at times of conflict and these too, can be an escape. A habit of escaping from conflict is easily formed and can lead to many different kinds of behaviour. People trying to escape from conflict can be withdrawn, manipulative or obsessed by some idea or person. They also sometimes develop physical symptoms or escape into drink or drugs.

Self-deception, which involves crooked or devious thinking, can be a form of escape from anxiety or conflict and is self-destructive. The thinking is usually self-protective or self-centred. A woman who is clearly doing her job badly may discount the criticism of her boss by persuading herself that he must be worried about other matters, thus hastening her own dismissal. A girl working for an examination may come to believe that frequent absence from class will make no difference to her results, and she may be genuinely astonished when she fails. Sometimes women take their husbands or boyfriends so much for granted that it does not occur to them that their neglect or difficult behaviour is jeopardising the relationship, and are genuinely astonished when this breaks down.

Sometimes the self-deception is even more extreme. Some people become adept at persuading themselves that something which clearly happened did not happen and it may be impossible to persuade them that it did. For instance, after a bitter quarrel or an episode of outrageous behaviour a woman may behave as though nothing has happened and expect everyone else to go along with this. Often this technique is surprisingly successful, particularly if the 'escape from reality' is done with skill accompanied by charm. But ultimately it is self-destructive. Many a husband and boyfriend puts up with this type of behaviour for a long time but eventually he despairs and retaliates or departs.

Another form of self-deception is transmitted from others, usually the group, the family, or simply the mother. The child's perception of itself or of the outside world is coloured by what it has been 'taught' to perceive, and as a result perceptions that accord with that colouring are received with appropriate inferences while perceptions that do not accord are disregarded or distorted. Such mechanisms are the basis of prejudice, of feelings of inadequacy and also of much hysterical behaviour. Thus a woman with a great need for violence, both physical and verbal, created in her two small daughters a tremendous fear of their father, from whom the mother assured them she would protect them. Meanwhile she constantly goaded her husband and did all she could to provoke him to some form of violence. He was basically a peaceful man but the rare occasions when he responded were used by the mother to reinforce the little girls' terror until they could not bear to be in their father's presence. It was many years before he, and still later they, understood what had been going on. As long as they were trapped by this transmitted self-deception, which was really a form of brainwashing, they suffered severely from depression, feelings of futility and, not surprisingly, they had difficulty in forming relationships with men.

Withdrawal is a common form of escape and can lead to serious self-destruction. Apparent physical illness is often a form of withdrawal, perhaps from an inability to face competition or some other feared situation. Sometimes the withdrawal is a subtle and hostile form of non-participation, as in the case of a young woman on a visit to her future in-laws. During the visit a French couple who spoke no English arrived unexpectedly, friends of one of the daughters. The whole family sat down with them and tried to make them feel at home, struggling at having to switch suddenly to their imperfect French. The young fiancée sat silently throughout, and the family assumed that she did not understand the language. Later it turned out that she spoke excellent French and had even worked as a translator. Not surprisingly they felt humiliated and angry. By her behaviour the young woman had damaged her relationship with them.

Withdrawal as a form of escape can be total. At the age of thirteen Jean felt confused about herself and in touch with no one. Her parents seemed remote and demanding, her school made no sense of her. She was terrified by the changes and conflicts of adolescence and in anything to do with sex she was both ignorant and fearful. Her parents were puritanical and did not discuss such matters and the school was strictly religious. Jean felt she had no one to whom she could turn. She stopped speaking and refused to go to school. Apart from occasional attacks of screaming she was silent for three years. She was taken to various psychiatrists, with whom she remained mute. She was diagnosed as schizophrenic and of low intelligence and even spent some months in a mental hospital. But eventually she developed into a charming young woman who proceeded to pass her O-levels, A-levels and then went to university where she did well and enjoyed herself. Jean nearly destroyed herself by her chosen path of withdrawal, but her emergence as an intact and productive person is an example of how sometimes even the most self-destructive people can find themselves and then develop as creative and positive people, often gaining much from their unhappy past.

Retreat from the world by taking excessive quantities of drink and drugs is one of the most obvious forms of self-destructiveness. It is usually an attempt to relieve anxiety and avoid conflict. Often it is a deliberate search for oblivion. There are usually hostile motives too, often against a husband, lover or children. It can be a means of showing the world how inadequate one is, and this, paradoxically, is often combined with hidden determination and ambition. Sometimes it is a means of showing anger and hostility that is otherwise too contained to reveal. It can be a conscious or semi-conscious self-destructive urge, a means of losing husband, job or self-respect, or even one's life. 'I shall drink myself to death', said one middle-aged woman, and proceeded to do so.

Many women, when faced with problems that seem intolerable or with conflicts that they cannot face, find themselves drinking more than is good for them or becoming dependent on sleeping pills, tranquillizers and antidepressant drugs, often in larger quantities than have been prescribed. Some deceive themselves into thinking that they are consuming only reasonable quantities. Others deceive their doctors, who do not always check on the quantity prescribed or the frequency of prescriptions. The most persistent of these women visit several doctors and do not tell them about the others.

Ruth was a talented art student who did well until, over a period of a couple of weeks, she became aggressive and disoriented. She had recently broken with her boyfriend but became convinced that he was going to marry her the following week. To keep her quiet, and because she was frightened of her, her mother went along with these delusions and even accompanied Ruth when she went to try on wedding dresses and deliver wedding invitations. Eventually Ruth smashed up the flat and attacked her parents with broken furniture. At this point she was admitted to hospital and a large quantity of drugs were found in her bag. After treatment she returned to normal and was discharged, but within two months the symptoms had recurred. It gradually emerged that she visited several different doctors, none of whom knew that anyone else was treating her. She obtained supplies of drugs from each doctor. In spite of several subsequent breakdowns and increased liaison between the doctors, she still managed to obtain drugs. Whenever she started taking them in quantity, she became aggressive and wild to the point of madness.

Some women manage to keep their drink and drug habits secret for years, especially if they have husbands who are careless in their habits or who themselves drink heavily. Joan was in her late thirties and had had many hospital admissions, mostly for broken bones, 'falling attacks', 'spontaneous bruising', and irregularities of heart-beat. She had been investigated by doctors in several countries, but either they had never discovered the cause or, as soon as they did, she moved on. During one hospital admission the possibility that a combination of drink and drugs was the cause of her symptoms was seriously considered. She strongly denied the possibility, but close observation revealed that the harmless-looking bottles of 'ginger ale' which she liked to keep at her bedside were full of brandy. Her husband, himself a heavy drinker, was asked to search the house and he turned up next day with a bag containing more than fifty bottles of tablets, including amphetamines which are stimulant drugs and are liable to affect the heart's beat. Eventually Joan admitted that she had been addicted to amphetamines since the age of sixteen. These drugs had become more difficult to obtain because of tighter legal control and the increasing reluctance of doctors to prescribe them. When deprived of them Joan felt 'awful' and unable to face life, so she had taken to drink as well. When she was given a regular supply of amphetamines, carefully controlled and counted, she improved. Although she felt unable to tackle her addiction, she was able to lead a relatively normal life, and to care for her house and children in a way she had not done for years.

Self-destructive escape often takes the form of physical symptoms. I am not, of course, implying that the development of physical symptoms is always, or even usually, a form of self-destruction, only that this is often so, especially when investigation fails to find the cause of the symptoms. Doctors customarily divide physical symptoms into those that are 'organic', or of psychological origin. Organic disease tends, of course, to be destructive, and some organic diseases are purposefully self-destructive or else the result of self-destructive habits and ways of life. Examples of these are some cases of 'smokers' cancer' and alcoholic cirrhosis of the liver. But functional physical symptoms are much more common and a high proportion of these are self-destructive in either origin or effect.

Many people suffer from back pains, neck pains, muscle pains, difficulty in swallowing, indigestion and so on, in ways that prevent them from getting on with their lives. These symptoms are often also forms of protest or self-protective manoeuvres. It is, for instance, often easy to discover what it is that the patient 'can't stomach' or who she regards as a 'pain in the neck'. Sometimes a more urgent form of self-destructiveness underlies the symptoms. There are people whose covert aim seems to be to have a surgical operation to destroy or remove some part of them, and if they are clever they may find this easy to achieve since many doctors reflect our organically-minded society, believing that there must be a 'cause' of the trouble which, once found, can be removed. Thus one sometimes encounters patients, usually women, who have had almost every removable part removed – tonsils, coccyx, spleen, knee caps, thyroid, teeth, uterus, gall-bladder, stomach and so on. Usually some of these operations have led to complications so that as time goes on the patient is likely to develop symptoms which are undoubtedly organic in origin and require further medical intervention. One might comment that such people lead a life of careful devotion to self-destruction.

Sometimes physical symptoms are part of a complex system of self-destructiveness, hopelessness and revenge. One example of this was Hilary, whose only escape and relief from the tension of her relationship with her powerful controlling mother was to wet the bed at night. This she continued to do into her teens, and the mother's response was to ignore it, for it did not form part of her view of her child. But she silently punished Hilary, as Hilary punished her, by sending the girl away to stay with friends and relatives without mentioning the girl's problem. Thus beds were ruined and tempers frayed, and the mother revenged herself upon the world against whom her outwardly 'perfect' daughter was her defence. But the person who suffered most was Hilary, a sad example of transmitted self-destructiveness.

Obsessions, unless very mild, are usually self-destructive forms of escape as well as defences against anxiety. This is true of all kinds of obsession. The obsession may be about an idea and lead to fanaticism, about a person and cause obsessional love or hate, or it may be a habit such as compulsive, repetitive washing of the hands, or constant checking of small details such as locks, light switches and gas taps. There may be compulsive routines, such as cleaning the house constantly and excessively, or rituals, such as having to dress in a particular, highly detailed way, and having to start all over again if something interferes with the ritual. In extreme cases there may be endless apparently meaningless actions which have to be performed, such as tapping the foot seven times before entering a room. Such compulsions tend to multiply so that the necessity to tap seven times becomes seven times seven and then seven times seven times seven and so on, until the whole day and the whole life is taken up with the process.

These last are forms of obsessional neurosis and are self-destructive in that sufferers are unable to get on with their lives. But lesser forms of obsession also tend to be self-destructive. Even if they do not limit daily life to an intolerable degree, excessive attention to detail and total concentration on a narrow field or a single person tend to kill spontaneous and creative impulses and to prevent imaginative activity, all of which are necessary to a productive life.

Idealization is a way of looking at something or somebody in which the good points are emphasized and the bad are denied. Children tend to idealize their parents, often separating the good from the bad. Part of the process of growing up consists in bringing the good and bad together and realizing that they are part of the same person. Failure to do this leads to lack of further development.

Many adults idealize their spouses, their children, their teachers. But this leads to Cloud Cuckoo Land. Janet's father died suddenly when she was ten and in the middle of the kind of love affair with him which is a normal part of the childhood of many little girls. She remembered him as perfect and even when, as an adult, she came across evidence that he had been financially dishonest and an inveterate womanizer, she refused to believe it. She spent her youth searching for a man as perfect as he had been. The objects of her choice were always much older than she. She never could admit that they had faults and, in turn, each man let her down. Each affair and two marriages ended with sudden disillusion and drama. It seemed as if she was forever repeating the experience she had had with her father, who had been so perfect and had let her down so suddenly and totally by dropping dead.

Close to idealization is pathological hatred, which might be described as the negative of idealization. People who have idealized someone or longed to do so sometimes reverse their feelings and develop excessive and unreasonable hatred. When she found that her husband did not live up to her expectations Audrey developed such feelings. She conducted a vicious and relentless vendetta against him. While making love she would wait until he reached a state of excitement and would then suddenly announce that she did not feel like it anymore and push him away. This habit, together with vicious kicks she gave him whenever he was asleep and she was awake caused him to move to another bedroom. She then refused to cook or wash for him or allow him to use the refrigerator or the washing machine.

She turned the children against him and even persuaded them to
throw stones at him. Eventually he left the house and went to live in a
bedsitter. She refused to allow him to see the children and dictated to
them letters of hate, which she then posted. After protracted court
proceedings, in which she tried to vilify him and to screw every
penny out of him, she defied a court order giving him access to his
children. When summoned to court to explain this she excused
herself on the grounds the children hated him and refused to see him.
In his summing-up the judge commented that no one who had seen
her in the witness box could doubt that she was imbued with an
overwhelming feeling of hatred for her husband which she would
try to put into action in every possible way. But the self-
destructiveness in her attitude and actions is shown in what happened later. Her husband recovered and made a new life for himself.
The children, as they grew up, came to see her for what she was.
They rebelled and joined their father, leaving her alone and embit-
tered.

Phobias are strong irrational fears. Fears and phobias are often a
means of escape, and they usually also have an element of aggression
and manipulation. An important criterion is what the fears and
phobias prevent the woman from doing. A woman whose phobias
are confined to heights or thunder can probably carry on a normal
life, but if the phobia is for, say, cats or ambulances she is likely to be
severely restricted in what she does. She may not be able to go out in
case she meets a cat or an ambulance. If she suffers from agoraphobia,
the excessive fear of public places such as streets and shops, she has to
organize her life around this and probably the life of her family too.
Her husband may have to take time off to go shopping with her and
if her children are small she may be unable to take them out and if
they are older they may feel guilty if they do not accompany her
everywhere. The aggression and manipulativeness is not hard to see.
Her destructiveness towards others tends to turn against her and she
herself is also prevented from progressing. She may be unable to take
a job, travel on public transport or go to the library. Her phobia
gradually swallows her and she loses such sense of self as she had
previously possessed.

Hysteria, like phobia, is a means of escaping from conflict. It is a
disorder in which physical symptoms or certain mental disturbances
occur without physical disease. The symptoms are the result of an
unconscious attempt to avoid specific conflicts and they protect
against the anxiety of real situations or unacceptable wishes and
fantasies, which are also unconscious. Thus a young woman who
had committed bigamy went to a dance hall with her new husband
and saw her first husband in the far corner. She was immediately

stricken with paralysis of the legs so that she could no longer move forward and face the situation. A girl of twenty, who already had four children, was also stricken with paralysis which kept her in bed for years, thus successfully avoiding the necessity of caring for her children or incurring further pregnancies. Loss of memory after an unpleasant experience or after committing a crime is also a fairly common example of hysteria.

People who do not necessarily go in for such dramatic forms of hysteria but who habitually employ methods of unconscious denial and falsification of experience are said to be of hysterical personality, and this too can be self-destructive. One must emphasize the words *habitual* and *unconscious,* for most people behave like this sometimes. To realize this one only has to listen to opposing arguments about what happened in a traffic accident.

It seemed to Fiona's husband that she was incapable of telling the truth. She would say that she had come home at four when he knew she had come back at five and that she had read four books when she had read only one. She told him she had knitted a sweater when she had only knitted one side, that she had got a job when she had only applied for it, that she had won a competition when she had merely entered for it and that she had only one whisky when the bottle was empty. But Fiona was not telling deliberate lies. In whatever she did her first impulse was to distort the truth and falsify her experience to what she would like to be true. It affected every aspect of her life and so prevented the normal testing of self and fantasy against reality that is the basis of progress. Not surprisingly, Fiona remained incompetent in her life and immature in her relationships. There are many women like Fiona.

Manipulativeness is closely related to hysteria, and it is useful to look on hysterical behaviour as a form of manipulative manoeuvre. Manipulation is doing or saying something with an underlying motive which may be conscious but is often unconscious. The underlying motive may be to let loose some form of aggression or envy, to make the other person feel humiliated or guilty or unworthy. Bitchiness is a common form of aggressive manipulation designed to humiliate or injure another person. Emotional blackmail is another form. Manipulativeness may be directed towards some event such as marriage or pregnancy or a change of house or the purchase of some desired object. Some degree of manipulativeness is part of normal life, especially when it is benevolent. A certain amount of manipulativeness is generally regarded as part of a woman's stock in trade. Manipulativeness as such is not necessarily self-destructive, but if it is aggressive or self-seeking it usually has this effect because not only does it prevent development but it tends to cause retaliation by others, which is also often unconscious. Productive people with a strong sense of 'real me' tend not to be manipulative and to avoid others who are, so the manipulators often find themselves friendless and frustrated.

Aggression plays an important part in self-destructiveness. The word aggression comes from the Latin *ad-gradi*, meaning to march or step forwards, but it also means to attack. Definitions given in the *Oxford English Dictionary* all concern attack: 'An unprovoked attack; the first attack in a quarrel: an assault, and inroad' and 'The practice of setting upon any one: the making of an attack or assault.' This idea has been perpetuated by psychoanalysts, who tend to regard aggression as synonymous with destructiveness and to associate it with sadism. But, largely through the work of ethologists, the aggressive drive or instinct has come to be understood as protective, progressive, and even creative, and one can see that it is concerned not only with attack but also with drive, self-assertiveness, and satisfaction. In this sense it is not self-destructive.

So only some forms of aggression are self-destructive, and when they are it is often because of the responses they provoke. On the whole aggressive women are more likely to be self-destructive than aggressive men because women are not expected to be aggressive (except perhaps in defence of their young), whereas men are expected to be. A certain amount of aggressiveness is regarded as manly, whereas the same in a woman is likely to be regarded as unfeminine. This is probably why so many women convert their drive and self-assertiveness into hostile attack. When there is a lack of outlet for normal aggression, hostile forms of aggression tend to replace it, and these are often turned against the self, either directly by the aggressor herself or indirectly by provoking responses in others.

Aggression in women has been much discussed in recent years. Traditionally women were not supposed to be aggressive, particularly in their relationship with men. Many people of both sexes regard all overt aggression as unfeminine, and it is interesting that so many women, as well as men, equate the women's movement with unfeminine aggression, thus perpetuating the extreme 'bra-burning' image while ignoring all other aspects of this movement. Certainly the task of reconciling healthy aggression with the expectations of others is a problem to many women, whether liberated or not, and this conflict underlies much self-destructive behaviour.

Provocativeness is a common manifestation of self-destructiveness in women. Provocative women use their aggression to cause others to damage them. By their actions they invite physical or verbal attack, rape or even murder. One man described his wife as a 'murderee', by which he meant that she provoked murderous feelings in him so that he found it difficult to restrain himself. 'She makes me feel like shaking her and banging her head against the wall' said another man of his teenage daughter, 'yet all she does is stand and look at me.'

Provocativeness is often a step towards open attack. If the man can be provoked into performing an illegal act or behaving in a way that will later make him feel ashamed, it gives the woman licence for retaliation and open aggression.

Much self-destructiveness can be seen as a form of protest, rebellion or retaliation directed either towards an individual or towards the world in general. Self-destructiveness is often a response to frustration, humiliation, undesired control or some impossible situation. If it does not take the form of escape, it is often active and aggressive.

Self-destructive protest can be seen in some immature or attention-seeking behaviour. Suicidal gestures are often of this type and so are many acts of 'bad behaviour', especially in children and young people. These are also often rebellious. But protest and rebellion can also have progressive, constructive components. They can sometimes be seen as an attempt by the true self to establish itself against the forces of compliance. Negative rebellion tends to be more self-destructive. By negative rebellion I mean the tendency to exaggerate compliance, as in the child whose parents insist on tidiness and he 'rebels' by spending his entire day tidying and retidying his room, or the wife who submits to her husband's wishes and adapts to his life to such an extreme that she no longer has any life or meaning of her own and so becomes a burden to him.

Retaliation is an attempt to punish those by whom one feels injured. These are usually parents, spouse or, less often, children. A child may disappoint his parents by failing an examination or by 'getting into trouble' as an act of retaliation, particularly when he feels he has no other way of rebelling against them. Such acts are frequently also self-destructive for they damage the child's future. A wife may retaliate against her husband by damaging his career or by denying sex or by humiliating, hurting or over-protecting him. She may gain satisfaction from this but usually such manoeuvres damage her as well.

Suicide, the ultimate self-destruction, is less common in women than in men. Suicidal gestures are more common in women, and some of these are dangerous. Many women who 'attempt' suicide, however, take great care to do themselves no damage, and the gesture is then not physically destructive but an act of manipulation, a protest, or an attempt to gain attention, aspects which have been discussed already.

It is not uncommon for a woman to make suicidal gestures in a kind of Russian roulette. She probably will not die, but on the other hand she may, and there is the possibility of permanent physical damage. Such a woman may take a lethal overdose of drugs and then telephone someone to say what she has done, or wait patiently for the person she is certain will arrive and take her to hospital. She knows that help may or may not come soon enough. The penalty she pays may be not death but permanent brain damage. She may drive a car dangerously fast, perhaps already drunk, as though dicing with death. Sometimes the suicidal impulse is less active. She may provoke someone to attack her or else continue to use a car or a piece of electrical equipment which she knows is in a dangerous condition. Or she may simply wish to be dead. Accident-proneness is also common in such people. Sometimes the physical destructiveness takes the form of self-mutilation and the woman may slash her wrists or throat, or make deep custs and gashes on her arms. I have seen women who have carved messages on themselves such as 'Death' or 'I hate you' and these cuts, if deep, as they often are, may leave permanent scars. One woman wound elastic bands tightly around each of her fingers until they became gangrenous and dropped off. Less obvious forms of physical self-destructiveness are some forms of overeating and oversmoking – often done with desperation and a determination to damage. Seeking surgical operations is another form of physical self-destructiveness, and yet another is anorexia nervosa, a condition which afflicts mainly young girls and has been described as 'the relentless pursuit of thinness'. In severe cases, when not properly treated, these girls literally starve themselves to death. In all these conditions there is a good deal of aggression.

Self-destructiveness often reveals itself in social behaviour. A well-known politician persistently seduced his colleagues' wives and a doctor his patients. A man prominent in public life had had since childhood fantasies of being whipped, and sometimes he sought out prostitutes to put this into practice. In spite of his position and the fact that his face was known to the public, he began to walk round Soho at night, looking at notice boards and telephoning some of the women who advertised. He admitted that a partial desire both to spoil his career and his private life urged him on.

Social self-destructiveness is usually more subtle. People do it in ways that may seem silly. One woman sent a message to her boss excusing herself from attending an important meeting on the grounds that she was busy making herself a pregnancy smock. Another was dropped by all her friends in turn because she continually devised situations that depended on her and then let the others down at the last minute, always leaving them in an awkward situation. Bitchiness is a common form of social self-destructiveness and so is creating scenes, continually denigrating a husband in public, or withdrawing into the home and refusing either to give or accept invitations. Sometimes what looks like self-destructiveness, like other forms of self-destructiveness, is actually protective and positive. For instance a woman may give up all social life temporarily to concentrate on family and job, to write a book or simply because she needs time to herself. This is not self-destructive because it is done for a specific, productive purpose and such a woman is unlikely to have much difficulty in resuming relationships when time and inclination permit.

Control, and the necessity to control, are also important in the development of self-destructiveness. Erich Fromm, in his book *The Anatomy of Human Destructiveness,* records his beliefs that 'the essence of sadism is the passion for unlimited, godlike control over men and things', and that the core of sadism is *'the passion to have absolute and unrestricted control over a living being,'* and *'the transformation of impotence into the experience of omnipotence'* (his italics).

The desire to control people is often a defensive substitute for inner emptiness that lacks joy and productivity. In this sense it is self-destructive or a manifestation of self-destructiveness. Such people are neither progressive nor imaginative and they damage or destroy these qualities in others.

In ordinary human relationships the person who needs to control is usually matched by a person or people eager or willing to be controlled. The traditional submissiveness into which so many women are raised means that usually it is the wife who is controlled and her husband who is the controller. But many women with the urge to dominate and control do so in a hidden, often indirect way.

Just as common, and perhaps commoner than desire to control people, is the desire to control things and processes. Obsessionality is an aspect of this. It has been described as the desire to gain *total control over a limited environment,* and one can often see it as such. Typical would be a woman whose house and children are exceptionally clean and tidy but who has no other interests, or one who maintains total order in her office but little interest in what the office is achieving or in any life outside. Such people are not, on the whole, productive. What is important to them is the process rather than the product.

Many people fail to achieve or to satisfy themselves because they are perfectionists. They feel that if they cannot do something perfectly it is not worth trying. Or they refuse to attempt something new for fear that they will not be able to achieve the high standard that they persuade themselves is necessary. This kind of thinking is closely related to a lack of self-confidence. It is very limiting to the personality.

Even the most normal, developed and productive people have elements of self-destructiveness in their natures and may go through periods of marked self-destructiveness. A number of such people have already been described. A certain amount of self-destructiveness is part of normal development and the person who has never shown any is probably overcompliant and therefore actually suffering from a severe form of self-destructiveness. I feel sure that anyone who has read this book so far will recognize parts of themselves and of other people they know. Sometimes a temporary period of self-destructiveness occurs until a more productive solution to a predicament can be discovered. Sometimes a form of self-destructiveness is a protection against something far worse. Sometimes it is a question of *reculer pour mieux sauter,* a preparation for better things. The value of self-destructiveness will be discussed more fully in the final chapter.

Chapter Six
Feeling and Fantasy

Self-destructive behaviour, like much other behaviour, is based on feeling and fantasy, chiefly concerning oneself and one's relation to the outside world. Self-destructiveness comes from feelings of emptiness and hopelessness, unreality, futility and lack of motivation or sense of 'real me'. These go with fantasies about one's lack of value, uselessness and unworthiness, of being compliant to outside demands, and often feelings of guilt.

In a world that has so much to offer to women it may at first sight seem strange that so many should experience self-destructive feelings for so much of the time. In a society in which women have more opportunities than ever before it seems paradoxical that self-destructiveness is increasing among them and is apparently more common in them than in men. Yet most people are aware of the possibility of self-destructiveness in themselves and actually behave self-destructively in some way or go through periods of so doing. It is clear that some situations tend to provoke such behaviour, particularly those in which there is anxiety, frustration and in which the environment makes unwelcome demands, or potential demands, or impinges in some other way. Other situations seem to come from within a person's mind and are either too difficult to cope with or else follow a pattern of conflicts that occurred at an earlier stage of life. In tracing a person's detailed life history one can usually see how and when the self-destructiveness developed and why it has formed its particular pattern. It is not always clear why apparently similar situations and difficulties should provoke self-destructiveness in one person, appear to have little effect on another and in yet another act as a spur to development and productivity. But human beings are complicated, and in a single person multiple character traits can combine and conflict so that the influence of single events or situations becomes difficult to see. Hereditary influences as well as acquired strengths and vulnerabilities affect such differences. Some people may be constitutionally more or less able to sustain or benefit from the stresses and strains that are inevitably part of life. Early experiences strengthen or weaken constitutional tendencies.

The worst forms of self-destructiveness are often found in people who appear to have considerable advantages in life and the best opportunities to make of it what they will. A striking example of this is anorexia nervosa, which has recently become epidemic among young women in the western world. This condition is virtually confined to girls from the more prosperous sections of the community and is unknown where food is difficult to obtain. Where living is a question of sheer survival, people tend to be far less self-destructive. When faced with a real crisis, many self-destructive people rise to the occasion and cope admirably. But, given freedom of choice and opportunity and the things they believe they want, many people are unable to make anything of their lives. Instead they live miserably while making others miserable.

It seems that self-destructiveness is encouraged by the very things people strive for and achieve. Once the exigencies of reality are removed, fantasy takes over. Fantasy probably always contains elements of aggressiveness and self-destructiveness and if these are powerful they may be put into practice. Everyone goes through life with a conscious stream of fantasy. To recognize this one has only to follow the activity of one's mind when one is doing nothing in particular. Except when the mind is concentrating on a specific task, the thoughts roam, sometimes along concrete or practical lines but often in highly personal and even bizarre ways. We all have unconscious fantasies too, which may or may not sometimes come into consciousness. Often other people are more aware of these fantasies than the person who has them, especially if those others are perceptive or trained in the art of following unconscious fantasies.

People attempt to balance their feeling and fantasy with what they perceive in the outside world. A child who feels unloved tends to behave in an unlovable way and then feels that the results of this behaviour 'prove' the 'truth' of fantasies that he may not even know he has. A woman of low self-esteem tends to behave in a manner which demonstrates her unworthiness and which reveals her lack of self-respect. This is the background of much self-destructive behaviour, especially in women.

Our society, despite recent changes, still tends to allot females a separate, often subservient rôle, and still extols the virtues of traditional female submissiveness and passivity, while at the same time demanding that women be sex-objects and also equal with men. It is hardly surprising, therefore, that so many women esteem themselves so low, or that when given opportunities to escape and make something of themselves, they are unable to take these opportunities and instead resort to behaviour which fits their fantasies. But there are enormous differences between individuals and these do not always seem to accord with their experience of life. In most self-destructive people one can trace disastrous experiences in early childhood, particularly continuous experiences, which have become associated with lasting feelings of futility and lack of a sense of self. Yet it is not difficult to find people who have had the grimmest of early lives and yet have survived without being either destructive or self-destructive.

Mary's mother was alcoholic, neglected her when she was a baby, and committed suicide when she was five years old. Mary was brought up by a dour, resentful father, from whom she inherited a crippling and disfiguring disease which made it unlikely that she would ever marry. Her father refused, on the grounds that she was not worth it, to allow her the education for which she craved and which would have done justice to her intelligence. Never having known human warmth and support, deprived of training and social experience, and barred from most jobs because of physical disability, Mary proceeded to make a good life for herself, and developed a facility for seeing where she could be useful and find satisfaction. At the age of fifty she lives alone and has many friends and many interests. She is not at all self-destructive.

Molly's unmarried mother had handed her over in early infancy to the Foundling Hospital. She knew nothing of her origins. Throughout her childhood she slept in a large dormitory and was cared for by a series of paid and voluntary helpers, who emphasized the dependence of their charges and frequently told them how unworthy they were and how lucky it was that they were fed and clothed at all. A slow developer, she was not one of the lucky few who were selected from the orphan school to go to grammar school and at the age of fourteen she was sent as a scullery maid to a large, rigidly-run house where she was starved, degraded and given half a day off each month. When war was declared she joined the army where she did extremely well, became an officer and travelled widely. Afterwards, with clever manipulation of her lack of qualifications, she went to university. Now also in her fifties, she is happily married, holds a responsible and well-paid post in a big industrial organization, and has many outside interests.

Both Mary and Molly have, through all their difficulties, developed and retained self-respect, along with a strong sense of self, believing in themselves and in others. They balance these feelings and fantasies in the way they live their lives. One cannot help wondering why, with so many difficulties, they have been successful when so many others, apparently more fortunate, fail.

Feeling and fantasy about oneself and one's relation with the world have many aspects, and these, too, tend to balance each other. There are, for instance, feelings and fantasies about personal origins, power and position, family and other people, and about traumatic experiences, personal aspirations and love. These and many more, conscious and unconscious, make up one's inner life.

Feeling and fantasy about personal origins are often powerful. They centre on family background, the circumstances in which one came into the world and spent one's early life, and the influences of these. Some people have strong feelings about their personal origins and are aware that their lives are greatly influenced or even dominated by them. Others seem neither to care nor to be aware. Ideas and feelings about personal origins may be based on fact, hearsay, inference or pure fantasy, and are usually a mixture of these. Whatever their origins, they are intimately related to the presence or absence of self-destructiveness and the form it takes. Thus a woman who felt that she had only been conceived in order to be a servant and doormat to her parents frequently behaved in a degraded manner. She was often drunk and abusive towards her husband. She neglected her children. She stole money and drink from her family and neighbours. Sometimes she neglected herself by failing to wash or change her clothes so that she became physically offensive. All her behaviour seemed to be directed towards inducing people to despise and degrade her.

Another woman's fantasies from childhood were of being Daddy's little pet and all her life she felt that she could only function with the aid of a big, strong man. She did not really believe that she could do anything on her own. She married a man much older than herself and transferred to him the attachment and dependence she had felt for her father. When her husband died she tried to cast her son in the rôle of the strong man in her life and his refusal to play the allotted rôle precipitated a series of self-destructive acts, including three serious drug overdoses and two incidents of wrist slashing. This woman's self-destructive behaviour was highly manipulative, designed to obtain and keep the strong man on whom she felt her balance depended. Yet another woman's manipulative self-destructive behaviour turned out to be related to a terror of the dark which she felt went back to the days when she was imprisoned in a cot. She felt that this fear had become the basis of her whole life. She also felt that her terror must at all times be concealed. She had so ordered her life that never once had she been in a house or flat after dark without the presence of someone older than she and this had become an overwhelming necessity. Organizing this without admitting the origins to anyone became a dominating problem after her marriage

broke up and her husband left her with three children. She would go
to any lengths to ensure that she was never alone with them after
dark. Although she had a house of her own she never slept in it unless
she could persuade some adult to share it for the night. To this end
she picked up men and took them home for the night. She indulged
in behaviour that seemed self-destructive but also highly bizarre and
suggested total loss of self-respect. Her desperation led to incidents
involving doctors and hospitals, police, social workers and innumerable relatives. She would create incidents in order to get people to
come to her aid, but never mentioned that the basic cause was fear of
the dark. This fear led to her returning repeatedly to the house of a
violent, unstable boyfriend who beat her up frequently, turned her
out of the house nearly as often, and could not be trusted in a room
alone with her children because he beat them or assaulted them
sexually. She would take drugs and poisons to make herself too ill to
leave. She felt that her whole life depended on not being alone after
dark but that, at the same time, this fear must be concealed.

Feeling and fantasy about personal origins may go back to conception. A woman may be influenced by the knowledge or feeling that
she was conceived in a castle in Spain, or in Timbuctoo, as the result
of a drunken sexual assault on her mother, or in the middle of an air
raid. One woman was conscious that hers had been a virgin birth
(her conception had occurred without penetration and was followed
by a Caesarian birth). She felt 'different' from other people whose
birth had been less unusual. Some are influenced by feelings they
attribute to their parents, such as being a much wanted or unwanted
child, or being the sex or character that was desired or not desired.
The mode of birth can also be felt to be important, for example a
precipitate birth ('always in a hurry'), a breech ('the wrong way up'),
or a forceps delivery ('dragged unwillingly into the world'). I have
known two cases of women who were undiagnosed twins born, to
everyone's surprise, after the birth was thought to be complete. One
of these always felt that the whole process had been for her sister and
that she was of no consequence.   The other radiated the joy of her
parents when, after the arrival of their fourth boy, the longed for
daughter made her unexpected appearance. The actual day or date of
birth can be important too. Some people take pride in having been
born on 'the first day of spring' or on St Valentine's Day, or they
may feel privileged or cheated to be a 'leap-year baby', or conscious
that 'Wednesday's child is full of woe'. Others may be acutely
conscious that their mothers' health was ruined by their birth, or that
father deserted because he could not bear the crying baby or else used
his children to enhance his own image.

We all tend to pick on incidents and situations in our past, whether

remembered, related by others or imagined, that seemed to be
important to us. Those who have no such recollections are almost
certainly repressing them. These incidents and situations may or
may not have been influential in themselves, but they are important
because they symbolize the way we feel about ourselves. Unpleasant
incidents of this kind are often called 'traumatic experiences'. We
may feel that certain troubles stem from a frightening event, such as a
sexual assault or being beaten or left alone in the dark but, in truth,
unless the experience was exceptionally severe, most of these incidents are probably not influential in themselves but symbolize feelings that were already present, though hidden. In other words, they
brought unconscious fantasy into consciousness.

People who were adopted in infancy or who were very deprived in
early life, such as Molly (see p.73), often have particularly strong
fantasies about their unknown origins. These fantasies may be un-
bearable, and so tend to be unconscious, while the person professes
indifference to them. But many people with such backgrounds are
intensely interested and long to know the truth. Due to a recent
change in the law, this is now easier to discover. Some people go to
immense trouble to uncover their origins and devote years to the
task. It is in a sense the search for 'real me', a means of separating
themselves from their fantasy of 'real' parents, and is by no means
confined to those who were adopted or otherwise uprooted. Geneal-
ogy is a flourishing hobby. Many normal children with ordinary,
stable backgrounds, go through a stage of fantasizing about being
changelings. Adults, too, have fantasies about being descended from
royalty, brigands or ancient families.

Much feeling and fantasy centres on those things which were
concealed or which were presented as other than what they were.
Freud discussed this in terms of what he called 'the primal scene', the
parents' sexual intercourse from which the child is excluded, but this
is only symbolic of everything that goes on behind our backs or
which has been distorted in its presentation.

Sado-masochistic fantasies of inflicting pain or having it inflicted
are so common that it is sometimes said that everyone is basically
either sadistic or masochistic. In my experience many people are
strongly both and so sado-masochotic, some of them mostly sadistic, others mostly masochistic, whereas many people have few fantasies of either type. Sado-masochistic fantasies are not confined only
to sexual matters.They extend to human relationships in general and
to questions of power. Control over others is the hallmark of sadism,
and being overwhelmed or punished or else being a leader of others
(as opposed to controlling them) is the basis of masochism. Sadistic
qualities are associated with traditional masculinity, while the tradi-

tional woman has to be intensely masochistic to live up to what is expected of her. It is, therefore, not surprising that sadistic fantasies are found more frequently in men, whereas strong masochistic fantasies are at the root of much female self-destructiveness.

Closely related to sado-masochistic fantasies, and much influenced by them, are the fantasies which occur in situations of love and attachment. For many reasons love and attachment are subjects of endless fascination. They concern all of us, even if only by their absence. They mean different things to different people and often different things to the same person. Their complexity stems from an accumulation of feelings and fantasies stretching back to earliest experiences. Moreover, the fantasies underlying love and attachment are often not what they seem. Most literature, particularly poetry, on the subject of love tends to concentrate on certain types and aspects of it. Popular views echo this in simplified, even more idealized forms. In particular, love as the root of self-destructiveness is only portrayed occasionally, usually by artists of exceptional perception.

Feelings of attachment leading to love begin in infancy. Babies become attached to their mothers and to others in their immediate environment. They cling and do not like to be separated. They become dependent on those to whom they are attached and look to them for the satisfaction of their needs and demands. They yearn for them when they are absent and they explore means of keeping, manipulating and controlling them. They also develop feelings of hostility and frustration towards those to whom they are attached. They experiment, to see how far they can control their loved ones before they are themselves controlled. They also seek to please. Conversely mothers and others become attached to babies, seek to satisfy and please them and to provide for their needs. In these early forms of attachment lie the basis of human relationships and of later attachments and love. To increase our understanding of the roots of self-destructiveness it can be helpful to view adult forms of love and attachment as extensions of infantile forms. This does not imply that adult love develops directly or exclusively from what has happened in infancy. But, in spite of the undoubted importance of later experiences, most forms of adult love and attachment can be seen as extensions of normal infantile attachment or as inversions or perversions of this.

Love and attachment mean different things to different people. Even among people who pay lip-service to the currently popular ideas of 'love' or 'being in love', love can be utterly different both in its manifestations and in the feelings and fantasies behind these manifestations.

Types of adult love which seem to be the most direct extensions of normal infantile attachment involve being succoured and cared for by someone who is totally dependable, often in an exclusive relationship. Sometimes the need is simply to have someone around, even though not doing very much, and this may be extended to a number of other people. Middle-aged people especially often depend on having the whole family about them rather than just a spouse. Sometimes the elements of infantile attachment are less peaceful, with someone perpetually unsatisfied, forever seeking the boundaries of the relationship and pushing it to its limits, or else ignoring boundaries between one and the other, through a need to be totally wrapped up in the other person, virtually taking him over or being taken over by him. Sometimes the elements of infantile attachment are inverted so that the attachment is seen, not only as caring in the sense of being involved, concerned and identified, but as caring in the material sense of looking after, doing things for, and administering to needs. This type of inverted infant attachment is particularly common in women and is the origin of the male saying 'If a woman wants to cook meals for you and mend your shirts, she's after you.' Many lasting marriages are made on the basis of the prolonged infantile attachment being succoured by inverted infant attachment. The inverted, 'caring' attachment is not always seen in the woman. In some marriages a strong and stable man cares for and looks after his weak infant-wife.

Other forms of love and attachment can be seen more as perversions of the infantile, and these are particularly liable to become self-destructive. For instance, many are narcissistic, based on self-admiration. Being admired and indulged, receiving constant attention, and making big impressions, can all occur in the normal course of infant development. To a certain extent they may be essential to normal development, but in excess they lead to deformations of character that can become basic to the personality. Such a person grows up self-absorbed, incapable of loving anyone other than himself or herself. Much of the interaction in such a person's attachments and love life can be seen as efforts to gain admiration and to enhance self-love. This often goes with a series of seductions, feelings of conquest, a boosting of the self (so lacking in internal resources that it needs constant enhancement from outside) and frequently, endless search for novelty. Don Juan is a typical character of this sort, loving only himself, a prey to unfortunate women whose low self-esteem leads them to fall for his flattery and join him in his admiration of himself. Narcissistic women are also common, often attended by a devoted spouse and a host of other male admirers anxious to join her in her self-adoration. Such women are often physically attractive, for not only do they spend a great deal of time on their appearance but natural good looks often attract the kind of attention that accentuates narcissistic tendencies. Thus physical attractiveness and narcissism often enhance each other.

More extreme perversions of infantile attachment can be seen as sadistic, masochistic and compliant. Sadistic tendencies are basically efforts to control. Sadistic women like to control their relationships, often by narcissism and bitchiness. (Although men can be bitchy, the word *bitch* is of course female.) Controlling and degrading those who are attached to them is the basis of sadists' *modus operandi*. The satisfaction of seduction is often sadistic in origin and so is the demand for constant stimulation. Self-control is also often marked in those with sadistic tendencies, for the sadistic fantasies that underlie them tend to be unacceptable to conscious thoughts. Sadistic women, because they love power and tend to be self-controlled, often reach positions of responsibility or seek jobs which give them power. Although they are probably a small minority of all women, they tend to appear among receptionists (especially in places, such as hospitals, which do not need to encourage their customers), teachers, nursing sisters and traffic wardens. They tend to be labelled as 'dragons', they throw their weight about, they put down, with obvious enjoyment, those in their power and, because they lack traditional female virtues, they are responsible for the myth that women should not be given power.

Masochism is much commoner than sadism among women. Traditional female virtues are masochistic. Being controlled by others, especially by husbands, putting up with what comes, submitting to attacks and demands, always being in the background, and longing to be overpowered and conquered is still what many girls aim at and what is still regarded by some as what they should aim at. Most societies, including ours, tend to invert the original infant attachment in girls and convert them into caring, submissive wives and mothers. This can lead to masochism, especially in those with little self-esteem. Masochism easily becomes a way of life for the defeated and a refuge from the need for self-development. Such a way of life still has plenty of support from society, although less than formerly. This loss of support tends to turn women of this type towards self-destructiveness. There are still many down-trodden women, and women who insist on being down-trodden, who only feel comfortable in this situation and who know no other way of life. But there is less sympathy for them than formerly, and if they flag or complain they are less likely nowadays to be supported in their female lot and are more likely to be asked why on earth they put up with it, or simply given tranquillizers and sedatives by the doctor to keep them quiet.

Closely related to inverted infantile attachment and to masochism is compliance. Herein lies the root of much self-destructiveness in modern women. By compliance I mean feelings and behaviour which originate as a reaction to other people's demands, rather than as part of the true self. Conformity and the pleasing of others, which were formerly essential to acceptable womanhood, are still regarded as important. But the woman who today makes them the basis of her life at the expense of her personal development is liable to run into difficulties. Such a woman is incapable of taking opportunities, of developing personal interests or growing as a person. She is particularly liable to suffer when her supports fail: perhaps her marriage breaks down, her husband dies or leaves her, or children no longer need her. In these days of small families and easy divorce, any or all of these things are liable to occur when she still has half her life ahead of her.

These fantasies of self and attachment to others underlie the balance that each person has to find between the inner life and the world outside. They determine not only private feelings and the nature of relationships but also what each person does and hopes to do with his life. In any of these ways they can lead to self-destructiveness, which is an imbalance or maladaptation between private fantasy and the outside world.

Some people go through life with the aim of being as independent or as self-sufficient as possible. This may be a desire to break away from parents or to establish the true self in a way in which it can be satisfied and fulfilled with talents developed and used, or it may be a withdrawal from dependence and from close relationships, or an abhorrence of dependence. Some have fantasies dominated by the desire for control or mastery, either of themselves or of others. Such people may need always to be 'top dog', to pass their lives in constant acquisition, or to control others by making themselves irresistible, or indispensable to them. Others have passive underlying fantasies, such as of living exactly as their parents lived, bound up in compliance, submissiveness or vicarious living. Some are deeply involved in their own self-love, incapable of giving to others or of forming attachments other than those which enhance their self-esteem. Some feel they must endure what must be endured, or fill the void somehow or avoid anxiety at all costs.

All these underlying fantasies, whether conscious or unconscious, affect a woman in the way in which she plans, or does not plan, her life. Does she want marriage and children, or a career, or both? Does she have a drive to develop and use her talents? Does she prefer to be an empty vessel that can only be filled from outside or, frequently, not filled at all? In theory any of these possibilities are open to her within our society, but in any attempt to choose she will encounter conflicting pressures and influences, probably from herself and from outside.

Chapter Seven

Stages and Phases

It is not entirely clear where self-destructiveness begins or at what stage it afflicts females more than males. In this chapter I propose to develop ideas about the development of self-destructiveness which I discussed in a previous book *The Morbid Streak* and see how to apply them specifically to women in the modern world.

The doctrine of original sin implies that self-destructiveness is inherent in the nature of man. This view is less commonly held today than formerly, as is Freud's idea that the death instinct, the origin of self-destructiveness, is inborn. What seem to us to be true is that everyone has the capacity to become self-destructive. Self-destructiveness can usefully be regarded as a biological defence mechanism. Everyone at some time experiences pressures and anxiety. Mostly they cope with these constructively and are strengthened by the experience. But when they cannot react in this way they may be driven to self-destructiveness. For example, people confronted with serious business or marital problems may wrestle their way through to a solution, or they may give up and take to the bottle. People who take the latter course are likely to be already programmed to react to problems this way because they experience them unconsciously as impending and inevitable catastrophes. The potential catastrophe is likely to recede as life progresses but the fear, the fantasy, and often the anger remain, leading to inappropriate reactions left over from the past. This is often reinforced by a manipulative element which has produced gain in the past. Self-destructive behaviour tends to elicit concern and attention from parents and, later, from spouse, friends, doctors and so on, and this can be a powerful motive in self-destructive behaviour.

It seems probable that people are born with different capacities for becoming self-destructive. I believe that the ease or difficulty with which self-destructive feelings and behaviour develop and the form they take are profoundly influenced by inherited factors, although by no means wholly determined by them. There is as yet no scientific proof of this. My own belief rests on three arguments. Firstly, human characteristics that can be measured tend to be distributed in the population according to a so-called 'normal' curve. This means that their incidence or strength varies from very low to very high, most individuals being somewhere in the middle. This is also true where the effect of environment can be measured or discounted. Secondly, virtually any characteristic that can be assessed in animals can be encouraged or reduced by breeding techniques. This includes such vague characteristics as nervousness, docility, aggression, quick reaction and so on, and indicates the importance of heredity in such matters. There is no reason to suppose that man is different. Thirdly, certain people seem to defy common sense and turn out to be far more or far less self-destructive than one would expect from their circumstances. Although the environment often acts subtly and in different ways, it seems likely that certain individuals are by heredity stronger than others and can therefore survive adverse circumstances and traumatic experiences without severe damage while others, even when raised in more auspicious circumstances, become extremely self-destructive or are unable to withstand even the smaller stresses and strains of normal life. Furthermore, many people seem to be strong or weak in particular areas only and elsewhere react quite differently. They have weak spots, hidden vulnerabilities and variable strengths.

There is no reason to believe that, genetically speaking, girls are more liable to become self-destructive than boys. We know that boys tend to be weaker in health than girls and, except under conditions of exceptional medical and social care, they die more readily than girls. Certainly we must look elsewhere for the excess of self-destructiveness in women as compared with men.

It may be that the anxiety which underlies all self-destructiveness can begin before birth. Farmers and animal breeders have long recognised the importance of tranquillity and the bad effects of anxiety and traumatic experiences during early life, both before and after birth. We now know that certain experiences in early life, such as separation from the mother, her total absence, or aspects of her character or behaviour, can have long-term, often permanent, effects. We have recently begun to suspect that anxiety in pregnant women affects their unborn children in their later lives. Again there is no reason to suppose that the experiences of girls in the womb differ from those of boys or that their reactions to these experiences are different.

Self-destructiveness is uncommon in infancy and in any recognized form is probably only seen in the infants who suffer from severe emotional deprivation, for example, infants in institutions who are cared for by a series of nurses and have no opportunity to form attachments to individuals. Some of these infants tend to go into what Bowlby has called a state of 'detachment', eat poorly and may die. Infants who have good enough mothers or mother-figures do not do this. Nevertheless, much self-destructive behaviour in later life, particularly of the 'internal' variety which seems to spring from the person rather than from the circumstances, seems to have its roots in infancy. Many self-destructive people have unpleasant feelings and an awareness of emptiness and hopelessness which they know they have had since their earliest years.

The first environment after birth is the mother. In an earlier book, *Mothers, Their Power and Influence,* I described the ways in which the influence of our mothers determines the sort of adult we become and how this depends largely on the sort of feelings mothers have. Most mothers go through three stages with their children. In the first, they have the feeling that their children are part of themselves and enclosed within the same boundaries, even though they are actually separate. The second feeling, which comes a little later, is that the children are extensions of themselves. The third is that they are separate people. Some mothers may have one type of feeling most strongly and some another. Most feel a mixture which often varies, with different feelings predominating. Feelings of *enclosure* tend to predominate during the physiological stage of infancy when the child is totally dependent. The stage when feelings of *extension* predominate is the age at which the child is no longer a baby and is beginning to assert his independence. The third stage, *separation,* extends through adolescence into adult life. In the normal course of mothering each stage merges harmoniously with the one before and the one after, and it is impossible to draw an exact dividing line between any two stages. Most mothers cope with one stage more easily than another. What a mother *is* has much more influence on her child than what she *does.* All this has a profound effect on the potential development of self-destructiveness.

The first stage of motherhood, when the child is a baby and psychologically part of the mother, is probably the only stage through which the child can pass without developing self-destructive tendencies. If there is good rapport and a harmonious relationship between mother and baby, she will unconsciously meet the baby's needs and ensure that it is not forced to face conflicts beyond its capacity. In other words, with a good enough mother, a child learns to deal with discomfort and discontent in ways that are challenging but not overwhelming and which offer individual solutions rather than bland compliance. But this stage can also be the origin of the worst forms of self-destructiveness. If the mother cannot form that initial, vital rapport with the baby, or if she can only achieve a semblance of it through intellectual activity or expert advice, then the child's orientation to both itself and to the world around develop differently. This is because from this first stage come basic feelings about the world and the self, appropriate feelings of optimism and pessimism, of security and insecurity, what Laing has called 'primary ontological security', and Erikson has called 'basic trust', a sense of the need for vigilance along with the confidence and ability to relax, a sense of harmony and continuity, the ability to use imagination freely and to cope realistically with the physical world and with bodily feelings and functions. From it too comes the capacity for close contact with another person, both physical and psychological. To some extent the sense of curiosity and the capacity to explore new territory is also rooted in this stage of mothering.

The infant is at the mercy of whatever happens at this early stage. With no means of assessing what is taking place the baby absorbs whatever is available. Inevitably, what is experienced during this first stage will determine later relationships to the world and to other people. Trust and distrust, truth and falsity, acceptance and denial will all, as and when they occur, be 'built in' to his personality.

Many infants pass through this stage without difficulty and without having experiences liable to lead to self-destructiveness. But even when a mother is devoted she may not be capable of the feelings of the first stage. Or it may be that a particular infant is unable, for one reason or another, to respond. Whole cultures and sub-cultures can develop in which *enclosure* is replaced by *extension*. An example is the traditional upbringing that has long been found in the British upper classes. These can be highly successful but they are different from cultures in which *enclosure* predominates, for example in traditional Jewish or Mediterranean families. Any subsequent self-destructiveness also tends to be different. In a tradition that is predominantly one of *extension* during the early years, an infant is, almost from birth, directed and moulded in the way expected. As long as the environment is supportive the infant (and the child and adult it later becomes) may never be aware of discomfort. But if the environment fails, there is trouble. When that person, at whatever age, is thrown back on his or her own resources, or comes into conflict with the environment, latent self-destructiveness becomes apparent, particularly obsessionality, which is strongly related to controlling, and also depression, a lack of a sense of real me, and a sense of futility.

A common form of upbringing in the western world is that in which *enclosure* feelings are replaced by intellectual effort. This, as one would expect, is common among mothers who are educated or articulate and who use words as sources of power. The enormous success in the western world of Dr Benjamin Spock's *Baby and Child Care* was probably partly because a period of improvement in women's education was succeeded by a period of confusion about babies. Hitherto educated mothers had hired nurses to care for their infants. After the Second World War new discoveries about the mother-child bond coincided with the disappearance of servants and also with official encouragment of women to stay at home and look after their own babies, largely for political reasons.

Some women lack all feelings of *enclosure* and may freely admit that this is so. Their children may grow up with a sense of futility often preceded for many years by compliance for the sake of peace. There is often a strong element of denial of reality and the whole of life is lived within the mask of a false personality. This is the only way in which it is possible for such a person to feel comfortable and when the mask, for whatever reason, no longer serves its purpose, there is no comfort and often no cure. Many self-destructive people have backgrounds of this kind.

Yet some mothers have virtually no maternal feelings other than those of *enclosure*. They are incapable of ever really seeing their children as separate beings. Common, for instance, is a kind of smothering over-protectiveness that leads to a great deal of frustration and anxiety which may dog the sufferer throughout life and is at the root of much self-destructiveness. This kind of mothering is also the basis of many jokes about the 'yiddisher mama' whose main occupation in life is loving her son and whose only aim in bringing him up is that he shall love her. The self-destructiveness that often follows this kind of mothering tends to be overtly anxious and often involves difficulty in separating from home and becoming a potent individual.

In the mothering of infants and young children we can sometimes see differences between boys and girls. Most parents treat boys and girls differently in some ways, according to how they themselves were brought up or how they see society. Some mothers have a special desire or liking for or aversion to a particular sex. As one mother put it 'I was all prepared for a wonderful boy who would carry on my husband's name and do all the things we wanted him to - yet all I got was a puny girl.' While another mother longed for a little girl whom she could dress up and show off and was disappointed with her 'hulking, screaming boy'. Another woman adored her son because he reminded her of her dead father and disliked her daughter, who reminded her of herself. Such feelings can have a profound influence on the growth of an individual and greatly influence the development of self-destructiveness. But because they are infinitely varied it is unlikely that they can lead to the excess of self-destructiveness seen at present in women of our culture, though they may well do so of cultures in which the birth of a girl is regarded as greatly inferior to the birth of a boy.

The next stage is *extension*. This is usually the basis of the 'normal' and almost universal tendency to occasional self-destructive behaviour. As the child grows, inevitably its personal interests and desires clash with the restrictions imposed by the parents due to their feelings that the child is an extension of themselves and through the conflicts and suppression of conflicts that are inevitable in that situation. The stage of *extension* is sometimes aggressive. It tackles problems, attacks difficulties, grasps new knowledge. It destroys in order to build. Lack of extension in this sense is a denial of the reality of the world and therefore also a denial of self and of time. Lack of extension leads to difficulty in developing as a person because developing as a person requires a period of being an extension of the parent. Thus lack of *extension* leads to feelings of floundering, of being lost, of experiencing the world as futile and to self-destructiveness. But too much *extension* leads to rage, to problems of controlling and of being controlled, and again to living as a false personality.

Thus obvious self-destructive behaviour often develops as the baby grows into a child. It is frequently concerned with questions of control and being controlled. Food and toilet training are two areas in which mother and child often do battle, each struggling to control the other. The child often reacts in frustration and anger when there is a failure to recognize what he feels to be his needs. He soon learns the art of provoking parents and explores possible boundaries to find how far he can go.

It is useful to think of experiences that lead to self-destructiveness as forms of impingement. Anything that encroaches, that intrudes beyond comfortable limits, is an impingement. A pinprick is an impingement from without. A headache is an impingement from within. Impingement may give a feeling of being attacked or threatened, shut in or controlled. It may also give a feeling of being challenged, perhaps by a task that must be done, by something new and difficult or by some conflict.

A feeling of lack may be a sense of loss for something or someone, or it may be a feeling of never having had something that is needed. Lack can also be regarded as negative impingement. For instance, hunger is a form of discomfort due to lack of food, but it is experienced as the impingement of hunger pains. A sudden sensation of falling may be due to lack of support, but it is experienced as the impingement of unpleasant sensations. The impingement of feelings about what is lacking is often the cause, or at least the mechanism, through which the situation is experienced.

In *Inhibition, Symptoms and Anxiety* Freud wrote that missing someone who is loved and longed for is the key to an understanding of anxiety. Bowlby, who has probably spent more time than anyone else studying the subject of separation, thinks that Freud was probably wrong (*Separation*). But Bowlby believes that this kind of loss is common and leads to 'great and widespread suffering'. He divides the three stages through which a child goes when separated from his mother. First is the stage of protest, when the child is noisily and directly concerned with missing its mother. Then comes the stage of despair, in which the child is quieter but still preoccupied with the separation and experiencing grief and mourning. Last is the stage of detachment in which there are changes in the child, defences are built up which become part of the personality and the child is no longer directly concerned with the problem of separation. This is one of the points at which self-destructiveness emerges. Whenever feelings of impingement or lack are too great for the individual to master at the time destructive tendencies may develop.

Everyone experiences impingement and lack. Everyone dislikes extreme forms such as physical deprivation, hunger, thirst, fatigue or physical symptoms, being dangerously attacked or losing someone or something that is greatly loved or esteemed. But in everything except the most basic or extreme situations people vary so much in their feelings that there is often little common ground.

What is protective to one person and no source of discontent may be experienced by another as an intolerable impingement, and it may be either of these to the same person at different times. Loss to one person may be freedom to another. A challenge to one person may be a threat to another. People vary widely in their attitudes to different aspects of body structure and function and to such things as a naked body, to fatness and thinness, physical exercise, eating, sex (both private and public) and childbirth. In sensation and intellect they vary widely in reaction to, for example, stimulation or challenge, to the lack of these, and also to tension and anticipation, noise or being in a noisy atmosphere, being alone, reading and what is read, watching sport, experiencing dangerous situations, thunderstorms, spiders, art or imaginative activity.

It is in learning to deal with impingement and lack that we can see widespread, but by no means universal, differences between boys and girls. The mastery of impingement and lack can be one of man's highest achievements. Failure to master them is a source of self-destructiveness. Yet emphasis on mastery also encourages self-destructiveness and prevents the condition of imaginative receptivity that is harmonious, satisfying, creative and protective.

In our civilization there has long been much emphasis on mastery, particularly for males. This emphasis is usually stronger in Protestant than in Catholic countries. The idea that we must master our anxieties, grasp our problems and conquer our difficulties is strong both in puritan traditions and Freudian theories. But they tend to be linked in our culture with maleness, though there have always been individuals, such as Wordsworth and Keats, who saw things differently. Ideas of harmony and receptivity tend to be regarded as weaker than mastery and control and more suitable for females. The very word master has male connotations. Apart from control and mastery, other methods of dealing with impingement and lack are submission, protest, withdrawal, fright and avoidance. Apart from protest, these all tend to be encouraged in females.

Submission is the most immature method of dealing with impingement and lack. An unborn child, for instance, must submit to everything that happens and can hardly protest. An infant may protest but still submit. Submission in the sense of being overwhelmed is inevitable in a position of great weakness. Sometimes it is appropriate throughout life. Sometimes submission is the most appropriate reaction to, say, bureaucracy or to a dominant spouse. We submit for the sake of peace. But aberrant or unsuitable submission comes from intimidation or despair or the habit of these. The submissive person has, at least metaphorically, been defeated in the struggle and carries this beyond the circumstances of defeat. As a result part of the personality fails to develop. Self-confidence is lost, the future is killed, the way is open for self-destructiveness. Much the same situation is sometimes found in those who have been intimidated or controlled to an excessive degree. Here again they submit for the sake of a peace bought at the price of individuality, self-confidence and personal development. Someone whose personality is dominated by submissiveness is likely to have had experiences of this sort.

Closely associated with submissiveness is withdrawal, which is itself closely associated with flight and avoidance. Normal forms of these are often indistinguishable. For instance, withdrawal is often an immediate form of avoidance, as is also flight. On the whole withdrawal requires more mental activity than protest or submission. Flight and avoidance require still more. Each is suited to certain circumstances and they all tend to be used when there is no question of mastery and when there is no habit of mastery.

Beyond the child is the family and beyond the family is the outside world. Each family, community and society produces its own forms of self-destructiveness. Just as there are three types of mother who

regard their children as parts of themselves, as extensions or as
separate people, there are also three main types of environment:
cradling, directive and *unsupporting*. As with the three types of mothering they mingle with and merge into each other and no type is likely
to be found in its pure form. Nevertheless each produces its own
forms of self-destructiveness. The more obvious types of self-
destructiveness come from an *unsupporting* environment. *Cradling*
and *directive* environments can be almost totally supporting. When
this is so the individual may be totally adapted and compliant,
untroubled by self-destructiveness but limited in personality,
perhaps rigid or weak. As long as the individual has the enveloping
support of the structured system, self-destructiveness does not show
itself. In a world that changes rapidly the environment no longer
supports as it does when change is slow. When the needs of one
generation differ markedly from those of the last and the next,
environments that are purely cradling or directive are bound to fail,
and so become unsupporting and a potential source of conflict.
Difficulty in establishing independence, in separating one's own
from one's parents' wishes, may be a serious handicap. This is a
widespread problem today. Those who grow up in families whose
attitude is that children are parts or extensions of parents tend to
meet particular difficulties as they grow up in the modern world.
They often have a feeling of special security within the family and
may become self-destructive when required to make their way
outside in what is, for them, an unsupporting environment.

It is in the introduction to the outside world that the growing child
finds sex differences most marked. Society has probably changed
less for men than for women and many girls are brought up unpre-
pared for what they will meet. It is in the interaction between family
environment and the outside world that we first see good reasons for
the excess of self-destructiveness in women.

Children's first encounter with the outside world is at school.
Some become self-destructive early on, for they are unable to make
the transition from home to school. Sometimes the school is to
blame or is unsuited to a particular child, who may do well when
transferred elsewhere. More commonly such children come from
families in which there is emotional disturbance. Many have
mothers who have distorted personalities or who are depressed.
Some parents unwittingly induce a situation in which a child cannot
settle at school or even finds it difficult to go to school at all. Extreme
anxiety about incidents or changes at school, or about examinations,
usually originate in the home. Many children who fail to take advantage of their schools, or who are self-destructive in their attitudes
towards schools, come from homes in which relationships are dis-

torted or difficult, and their mothers are often themselves self-destructive.

Although self-destructive tendencies not infrequently become apparent at school, it is noteworthy that large numbers of children with little sense of self or 'real me' adapt to the school system, feel safe in the support of its conforming pressures and are often indistinguishable, except to the exceptionally discerning eye, from those of healthier development. Indeed, many of the worst cases, destined for adult lives of unhappiness, instability and self-destructiveness, adapt to school life without difficulty. Such children often do well academically, athletically and socially and they are often 'teachers' pets'. Compliance as a substitute for development of self suits the system of most schools and is inevitably encouraged. Those who do show self-destructive tendencies at school, particularly those who do this in a rebellious way, are often healthier, even though the teachers may not like them so much. Most school rebels are basically healthier than compliant children for they are striving to find themselves, are struggling against conforming pressures and feel shackled or unfulfilled by what is expected of them. Thus it is not surprising that many rebellious children turn into strong, surviving people, and many school conformists become inadequate, self-destructive adults.

It is doubtful whether the female predominance of self-destructiveness appears during the years of compulsory school attendance. Sexism, though less than formerly, is still widespread in schools, but this in itself does not produce self-destructiveness. Indeed it often prevents it by enabling girls to avoid the situations of choice that underlie so much self-destructiveness. There are still schools largely devoted to preparing girls to be good wives and which support them in this preparation. In such schools the problems of choice that tend to lead to self-destructiveness seldom arise. Instead, they are postponed. Similarly, in schools where girls are encouraged to make choices and to plan for their future as individuals in their own right, rather than as appendages to future husbands and children, there is usually a good deal of support, both in co-educational schools and those dedicated to the enhancement of higher education for women. In such schools working for examinations and planning for a career are accepted and expected and, on the whole, traditional virtues are not particularly encouraged. Whether a girl attends an old-fashioned school that aims to train good wives or one that believes in opportunities for women, the school creates a supportive environment. There are of course good schools and bad schools and there are misfits in both, and sometimes there is too much conflict between home and school for peaceful conformity, but on the whole it is only towards the end of their school careers and during the years immediately following that young women have to face real choices which, if they are to be successful, they have to make for themselves. Problems of specialization and training, choosing a career and obtaining qualifications tend to concide with emotional adolescent problems, sexual encounters and the need for new independence and social life. Thus it is in the adolescent facing the adult world that we often see the first outbursts of self-destructive behaviour. This is usually only a phase in healthy development, but it may be a manifestation of serious disorder.

Adolescence is the time when the young person, having absorbed the personalities and aspirations of the parents, has to branch out as an individual separate from the parents if personal development is to continue. To some extent this involves choosing which parent he or she wishes most to resemble and to some extent choosing what sort of person he or she is or wishes to be. Essentially it involves choice. Nowadays it is seldom possible simply to be like mother or father and to follow in their footsteps. To avoid the choice is to court disaster.

Many adolescents are incapable of making this choice. They tend to go straight on to university, training, job or marriage for no better reason than that this is expected or because it postpones decisions. Those who follow these patterns for such reasons merely postpone the crisis. Most teenage marriages break down and the universities are full of young people showing their first self-destructive behaviour. This often occurs near the beginning of the course in those who cannot settle, who are unhappy away from home or who have not developed the personal resources necessary for settlement as an individual in a new community. The other common time for self-destructive behaviour to appear is near the end of the course, as final examinations approach and prospects open of the frightening world outside the comparative safety of the university. Many young people break down or experience crisis at both stages. Some go right through the course or settle in marriage and have children without ever making the essential step to independence. They may be well into their adult lives before they realize the falsity of their situation. They may then find that they are trained for a job they do not like, or stuck with a husband whom they now find unsuitable or with children whom they wonder why they had, or wish they had not produced at such an early age, before they were able to emerge as individuals in their own right.

Women who have been through university or other training as a form of compliance often seek escape at this stage and the obvious escape for them is still marriage. They are unlikely to be much, if at all, better off than those who chose marriage earlier because it was expected of them. Their advantage is that they have degrees or other qualifications which may prove useful in the future.

Some people still manage to avoid these conflicts altogether and to pass their lives in a state of compliance. They may become self-destructive later, but often they pass their own averted crisis on to their children on whom, not surprisingly, they tend to put strong pressures for compliance. In their turn these children rebel or break down and the whole false facade is exposed. Although the parent seldom sees it in this way, the child or adolescent only recovers if he or she is able to understand it and to face it. Many adolescents understand this well and recover by becoming more adult and more developed than their parents.

In our society this crisis tends to be worse for women than for men because their rôle is changing and the guide-lines are fewer. In spite of all the changes that have taken place during the last generation, men are still generally expected to train for a job or profession and then to practise it, get married and raise a family. In spite of increasing voices to the contrary, they are not seriously expected to change or even adapt their work in order to raise children. That is nearly all done by women. Moreover the continuity of work for a man, and the prospects of change and promotion, make it in many ways easier for him to adapt it to suit his emerging personality, even if he had little individuality to start with. For example, a man who trained as an engineer or an accountant because it was expected of him may find that he is more suited to business or management and, if he is able enough, this transition is not difficult. He can change course within his profession and find satisfaction in increasing responsibility, status and pay. Such a course is seldom open to a woman. If she tries to devote herself to work she is likely to come up against the difficulties that women meet in the higher ranges of the professions, and in order to reach them at all she will probably have to forgo having children, or else will experience great difficulties in raising them. If she chooses to raise a family she is likely to put herself out of line for promotion and for the most interesting posts in which she would develop and fulfil herself. If she devotes, say, ten years to raising a family she can no longer compete with men for jobs because she will lack the necessary experience. She is likely to have to accept whatever work she is lucky enough to find. There may be none available for which she is trained, or she may by now have lost her self-confidence or her energy and feel unable to do anything except stay at home. Unless she is a vocational homemaker, she is likely to find this boring and unfulfilling. So, in a world of choice and opportunity for women, she feels she has no choice and is frustrated. She is unlikely to be supported by the community as women were in the past because there are now so many opportunities for women. She seems to be caught in a vicious circle, a situation which tends to bring out self-destructive tendencies.

So a young woman facing adult life is likely to be faced with many conflicting possibilities which she has to reconcile with a multitude of conflicting fantasies. She is likely to find herself in trouble if the possibilities do not accord with the fantasies, or if they only seem to do so. Balancing the world outside with how she feels inside is likely to be a formidable task, and though she may find practical support for whatever she chooses, society will not support her wholeheartedly. She may wish to become independent, self-supporting, skilled or successful. These ambitions are likely to conflict with desires for marriage, homemaking and children. Her main desires may be to marry and settle down but she may regret this later, or at least regret what she has missed. She may long for children but find it impossible to raise them happily. She may be steeped in traditional virtues desiring only to serve a strong man and to exist only through others, in which case she may suffer from lack of support and respect for others. She may be intensely narcissistic, desiring only admiration and a meal ticket, yet there are few niches for such women today.

Nowadays nearly all women work before they marry and most married women go out to work. Unlike a man, a woman may regard her work simply as a stopgap, not take it seriously, and give it up at the earliest opportunity. She may have a deep desire for dependence and opt for this rôle. Yet she will be aware of the increasing independence of women all around her, and of the increasing importance to them of work. She may take her work seriously, in which case marriage and a family will cause difficult conflicts.

Women often reveal latent self-destructive tendencies in their choice of husbands. One of the commonest types of marriage is still between a strong, controlling man and a passive, submissive woman. He may put her on a pedestal, but he still makes sure that he is in control. Such a marriage encourages the passive, submissive side of a woman and militates against her personal development. Such a woman may eventually 'grow up' and want something from her life other than ministering to a dominant male, or she may deny these needs and retreat into illness or break out into other self-destructive behaviour. At the other end of the scale many women who are independent and established have difficulty in finding suitable husbands for they are determined not to be controlled or to spend their lives ministering to others. Men who are prepared to enter an equal partnership, and who are not afraid of this, are still comparatively rare.

Nowhere are the conflicts of young women today seen more

clearly than in their attitudes to pregnancy. The fact that pregnancy has become a positive choice rather than a virtual inevitability has eliminated many problems but has brought others in its wake. More women than ever before are asking themselves whether they really want to have children and some are deciding that, on balance, they do not. Yet later, perhaps in their thirties, life often seems empty without children and they may change their minds and hasten to have children before it is too late. This is sometimes the result of personal change in development but it can be a means of filling emptiness.

Many women still deny the existence of choice and have babies automatically, as their mothers did. Having babies is a means of avoiding or delaying the choices that most women eventually have to make, and is one of the commonest means by which women try to escape from themselves. But rearing children today is difficult because our society, despite its lip-service, does not encourage them, is no longer geared to easy family life and in many ways positively discourages the bearing and rearing of children. Food and clothing are extremely expensive, housing is poor and often unsuitable for children, facilities are poor, there are few nursery schools, and schooling is often a serious problem, particularly at the secondary stage. Taxation is high. Domestic help is scarce. Society demands that mothers look after their children exclusively and the pressures to do this are psychological, economic and political. There are more highly educated and well trained women than ever before and this means that large numbers of women are not totally fulfilled by domestic life. Yet never has it been more difficult to be a mother without being a full-time mother for a number of years and dropping out of virtually everything else. Some of these women may find satisfaction in becoming involved in their children's activities, by, for example, serving the school. But many lack the desire to do this and feel frustrated.

Many women who manage successfully to become totally absorbed in their young families run into difficulties when the children get older and need them less. Their children have filled their lives for so many years and the increasing independence of these children leaves an emptiness that is difficult to fill. Some women insist that their children come home from school for lunch, simply so that they will not be parted from them for too long and to fill the empty hours. Later they may put intolerable pressure on their adolescent children to remain at home and not take full part in the world around them. They are really trying to solve the problem of their own emptiness and lack of development by trying to impose it on their children. It is when adolescent children rebel or leave home that women turn most frequently to self-destructiveness.

Middle age and the growing up of children is also often complicated by divorce which of course, has increased enormously in recent
years. Many women who thought that domestic life would be forever suddenly find themselves alone, and with little prospect of
another marriage. Not only are there far more women than men in
this age group, and increasingly so as age advances, but men tend to
marry younger women. Some women unwittingly create their own
divorces by their destructive behaviour, or else indulge in such
behaviour as a protest against loneliness. Many seek solace in alcohol
or become dependent on tranquillizers.

Old age may bring peace of mind or increasing self-
destructiveness. Few women whose level of personal development is
low enjoy their old age and many make life difficult for others.
Alcoholism, drug addiction and suicidal gestures are all common in
old women. Lack of inner resources is probably more difficult then
to conceal or to bypass than at any other age.

Chapter Eight

How Men Succeed and Fail with Women

The enormous changes which have affected women in our time influence every part of their lives, including the most important part, their relationships with men. Men have much to gain from women's new position and many realize this. But change tends to be threatening and many men, insofar as they are aware at all, are conscious only of what they will lose or, which is even more threatening, are afraid of what they might possibly lose. Under such a threat unacceptable feelings arise, and when this happens traditional views harden and male chauvinism emerges.

The word chauvinism is derived from the name of Nicholas Chauvin, a veteran French soldier of the First Republic and Empire. His demonstrative patriotism and loyalty were celebrated, and later ridiculed, by his comrades. Male chauvinism is the term now used to refer to exaggerated or inappropriate male outlook and behaviour in relation to women, based on the male supremacy of former times, particularly that which denigrates women, expects them to be subservient to a dominant male, denies them equality in matters that are socially rather than sexually determined, or turns them into sex objects. It may not be chauvinistic to open a door for a woman, but it is chauvinistic to expect her to stay behind it while the superior male pursues his own interests. It is chauvinistic to expect women to do all the chores and inferior work, to deny women work which they are able to do, to pay them less for similar work, to exclude them from sources of power and to choose them for their faces and figures rather than for their ability. It is chauvinistic to treat women as children, as though they were incapable of managing money or making decisions or had not a thought in their pretty little heads apart from clothes and pleasing men. It is chauvinistic to expect a woman to be totally fulfilled in cleaning her house and making life easy for her man, and to be always available when he happens to need her.

Some women thrive on male chauvinism, especially when it is

accompanied by gallantry, as it often is. Other women use it as a desperate defence against change. Probably most women like it at least sometimes or for some period in their lives. But, whether we like it or not, it is still part of our social life. Many women as well as men feel threatened by any other kind of relationship between the sexes. This is true even of some women who have become aware of themselves as individuals and have been profoundly influenced by the changes in our society. This is one of the important conflicts characteristic of the present time and often associated with self-destructiveness.

The interaction between men with male chauvinist fears and women floundering with seemingly impossible conflicts is the background of many relationships between people of opposite sexes. Such interaction creates much hostility, which may be either overt or latent, and is often converted into self-destructiveness.

The psychology of male chauvinism is varied in its origins and manifestations. Many insecure men feel that chauvinism is manly and reassures them about their identity and their masculinity. This feeling may be strengthened as women become increasingly strong and independent, for weak men then feel threatened. Only by denigrating women can such men feel safe. This kind of chauvinism is often practised in herds. Men gather together and do things without women, making a point of excluding them. Such men tend to choose women with whom they feel safe, and these women are submissive, traditional women, often doormats. These chauvinists often insist that their wives stay at home and do all the chores, or else that there is a strict division of labour, with the woman doing all the 'womanly' tasks, such as cleaning, cooking and washing-up, and the man doing the 'manly' tasks, such as mowing the lawn or painting the sitting room. Such men may even refuse to allow their wives to drive the car or to know anything of the family finances, and the women often feel safe in condoning this. If the man's insecurity is strongly sexual he may insist on marrying a virgin or be extremely jealous of other men. He often idealizes his wife and puts her on a pedestal.

Many women gain a great deal of security in such a relationship. The men appear to be strong but underneath the women recognize their insecurity, find satisfaction in it, and often have real, though hidden, power. Such a woman may proudly declare that her husband will not let her talk to any other man, or that she absolutely must have a meal on the table when he comes home, or that she cannot do the things she would like to because her husband would not like it. This kind of chauvinism also encourages women to use their energies and release their tensions by excessive and endless cleaning and cooking, as though having a nice well-ordered home and white washing is the height of, and the means to, self-fulfilment. This can also be used as a means of controlling the men or the children. These women's security comes not from being overtly dependent, but by making others dependent upon them. This is a kind of self-destructiveness which later often leads to more obvious displays of self-destructiveness.

This kind of chauvinism is still accepted as one of the norms of our society. The fact that it is accepted by vast numbers of people of both sexes is shown in its universal display. It is manifest any day in almost every newspaper, particularly the tabloids, in magazines, in children's reading books and in common parlance. It is worth noting that nearly every advertisement for food or household goods still portrays this kind of chauvinism. It sells soap powder, cigarettes, breakfast cereals and so on and is clearly successful in this.

Another type of male chauvinist was pampered by his mother and expects his wife to treat him in the same way. He has never had to do anything except earn a living and he believes that women exist to make him comfortable. He probably confesses that what happens in the house, even boiling an egg, is a 'mystery', meaning that by deliberately not knowing about such things he will ensure that he is well looked after. This makes him feel safe and important. Closely related is the narcissistic chauvinist for whom life is largely a question of collecting admiration. He finds a wife or a girlfriend who is willing to provide admiration in endless quantities. There is also the self-indulgent chauvinist for whom a woman is a means to an easy life. Any independence in her is a threat to his convenience and he will fight it.

Many men become obsessed with power and control, which is often a stronger force than sex. The power chauvinist controls for the sake of control. He may insist on knowing the household accounts down to the last penny. If his wife goes out he will want to know exactly where she is going, what she will do and at what hour she will return. Any hint of lack of control brings a terrible fear of loss of control which he suppresses by exerting even more control. Women seldom have the chance to develop this kind of personality themselves for they are even more excluded from the world of power and control than they are from the world of work. But they are often at the receiving end of it and minister to it unless and until they exert themselves against it.

Ambitious chauvinists need someone to help them on their climb to worldly success and many of them find that a wife is the best person for this. If she takes care of all the details and devotes herself totally to his career, he will climb further than he could ever do on his own. For some jobs, particularly political, diplomatic or overseas jobs in industry, such a wife is virtually a prerequisite. She is expected to follow him, move with him, minister to him, entertain for him and devote herself utterly to his career even at the expense of her children, let alone herself. The fact that she is seldom paid to do this is an indication of how powerful this kind of relationship can be. She is usually expected to be excellently groomed and well dressed, for her manner and appearance are an outward demonstration of her husband's position and success.

Lastly, there are chauvinists who have an underlying hatred of women and need to abuse or humiliate them. They tend to attach themselves to or to seek out masochistic women in order to denigrate them. They may pay prostitutes to be so humiliated, and this may be because the denigration they need to inflict is more than any woman in a normal relationship would tolerate. An example came to light recently in a case in which men in public life, while apparently leading impeccable family lives, were hiring prostitutes in order to defecate on them. Few men go to such extremes in acting out their fantasies, but many achieve it by metaphorically shitting on women in order to relieve their own tensions.

Each kind of male chauvinist tends to encourage female self-destructiveness in different ways, although they tend to do this passively by preventing or discouraging their women from developing. Most common is the traditional type of male chauvinist, who keeps his woman in her place by rigid division of labour and has little idea of her private and personal needs. Such men attract women of poor personal development who wish to have someone to hide behind. The suburbs are full of such wives, devoting themselves entirely to their families. They may attend coffee mornings and school functions and they may even play tennis at the local club in the afternoons, but they do nothing that interferes with their husbands' dominance and priority.

The over-mothered male chauvinist naturally atracts a 'motherly' woman. She likes to control by ministering and derives satisfaction from attending to his expectations and demands. The narcissistic male chauvinist is often a womanizer. He needs constant supplies of women, increasingly younger than himself, in order to gain the admiration he needs. He is likely, however, to demand total loyalty from his wife. Above all others, narcissistic chauvinists believe in the double standard, one for men and one for women. Any interest his wife may have in anyone else, or in any subject of her own choice, is experienced by him as a rebuff, even though he himself may have many girlfriends and outside interests.

The lazy, self-indulgent chauvinist is less likely to watch his wife or girlfriend so closely. As long as she ministers to him and gives him an easy life he probably does not enquire too closely into her other interests and activities. But he does not in any way support her in these.

The chauvinist who is obsessed by power and control tends to become more obsessed with these matters as he gets older. His wife probably feels that there is no contact between them, that he does not understand her at all, even though he professes to love her and strive for her well-being. In fact he is only able to comprehend her well-being insofar as it fits in with his personal power fantasies, so that he cannot comprehend that she might want something other than what he wants for her. Wives of power chauvinists often resort to self-destructive behaviour as an escape from the control of their husbands. Faced with alcoholism, drug dependence or suicidal gestures the power chauvinist loses some of his power. He only wants his wife to be well so that he can again control her as before. Her only escape from him is through her own self-destructiveness.

Chauvinists who have deep desires to denigrate and humiliate women often choose women with the lowest self-esteem, who feel they need to be denigrated and humiliated. Thus a vicious circle is formed. The more such a woman is humiliated the more she finds it necessary to submit to humiliation and behave in a degraded way.

At one time, and not so long ago, nearly all men were male chauvinists by modern standards because society demanded it and society supported such relationships. This is still true in many places and areas of life but, increasingly, it is becoming criticized and regarded as abnormal. Today women who marry male chauvinists do so from choice. They may be immature or unaware or fail to notice what they are doing. They may do it because it offers apparent security and allays, at least temporarily, problems in their own personalities, concerning their own identities and self-esteem. They may do it because of a deep-seated desire to be degraded. But increasingly such a choice is a self-destructive act. Thus women with self-destructive tendencies often choose male chauvinists as partners. When the relationship falters, the chauvinism then gives them an excuse for self-destructive behaviour. They can see no other way out of the relationship.

But male chauvinism can also be a powerful protection against self-destructive tendencies. When successful it can provide the support without which these tendencies emerge. It encourages compliance without the penalties of compliance. It prevents personal development and so negates the necessity for development. Many people can still pass their whole lives in this way. But it goes against the tide and all too often, as we have seen, the crisis occurs in the next generation.

Chapter Nine

Who Succeeds?

I started this book by asking why, at this time, when women have never had so much choice or such varied opportunities, so many of them are destroying themselves in ways both open and hidden or are failing to develop and find fulfilment.

The short answer is clear. More women who can cope with choice and change are enjoying their lives in our society than in any other society or any other age in the history of the world. But those who cannot choose or change are in jeopardy. Their lives in our society are often dreadful and to be dreaded. They hate the present and dread the future. They can neither make the choices they need to make nor adapt to the changes that they are liable to meet with accelerating frequency, and society as a whole does not help them. In general the family cannot help them either, for their inability to cope is usually rooted in the family. Many are conditioned by their parents to situations that would have been appropriate in a former age, and are still so in other societies today. But these are unsuitable to our own. Women caught in this situation tend to perpetuate it by choosing husbands who encourage or insist on values and patterns of behaviour that have become inappropriate. Thus new families are formed with ideas and attitudes which lead to self-destructiveness in the next generation and beyond. A psychiatrist may be able to help if he or she is not rooted in the psychological theories of a former age. The traditional Freudian view of women, with its emphasis on passivity and acceptance, is of no use to women with this problem and may make the problem worse. Even a psychiatrist who has an understanding of what is happening to women in our time – and a few with this understanding do exist – can only help a self-destructive woman if she can see the necessity to change and is willing to make a positive effort. But, since making a positive effort and trying to develop and fulfil themselves is what so many self-destructive women are conditioned most powerfully not to do, this may lead only to vicious circles.

In Chapter 2 we defined success and failure not in a worldly sense but in relation to how people feel about themselves. Success is a sense of making good with what one has, perhaps making the best of what one has. Being successful means being good enough in what one does or has to do. Deciding what is 'good enough' involves subjective judgment. There also has to be realistic appraisal, both internal and external, in which an individual's feeling and fantasy are linked to the external world. Paradoxically it is not difficult for most women to be successful in this sense in a world where virtually their only choice is traditional womanhood and in which there is little change from one generation to the next.

But our world is one of choice and change and these affect women even more than men. To be successful it is necessary first to be able to cope with choice and change. This requires above all else a strong sense of self. Those who have this can make choices and cope with change.

A sense of self is rooted in early experiences. Some people seem to develop it more easily than others. Although no one can influence her heredity or her early environment, nearly everyone has some sense of self, of what she is and what she really wants to do and achieve. This can be fostered or starved by deliberate intent, and by what is unconsciously transmitted and absorbed.

For a girl or young woman growing up today who wants to be able to enjoy her life and make the most of the unprecedented choices that are open to her there are several important steps. First, to develop her sense of self as far as she can, to be aware of the choices that lie ahead and to face them. The ability to judge what is or is not right for oneself is something that can be deliberately fostered by understanding and by observation, by being aware of how one really feels, and by using experience positively, however difficult or unpleasant that experience may be. This may mean going against what she has been brought up to believe. It may mean, as it often does, helping her parents into the new world. This may involve conflict, but if she can surmount this successfully she will benefit not only herself but also her parents, particularly her mother, who is also likely to be entering a difficult phase of life if she cannot cope with choice and change.

The second important step is to decide on things to do that are satisfying and fulfilling. Some of these should be lastingly satisfying, and adaptable to future change and choice. In practice this is usually most satisfactory if at least one of these occupations also brings in money. The capacity to be self-supporting is often as important today as a developed sense of self.

The third important step is to choose the right man, if she wishes, as most do, to be part of a couple. Many young women with an incomplete sense of self increase their difficulties by choosing men who will encourage their lack of development and extol their 'traditional' virtues. An inability or refusal to understand what is happening to women is common among women in our society, but it is far more common among men. This difficulty is particularly great because it is often concealed. A new relationship tends, and perhaps needs, to bring out romantic tendencies even in the most developed and level-headed people. A desire to serve the loved one, to cook and clean for him, mend his shirts and give up one's own interests for his may be a temporary and enjoyable phase in a sound relationship or it may be the preparation for a lifetime of slavery, lack of development and self-destructiveness. The type of person chosen and the relationship that develops will have a profound effect on personal development and the ability or inability to cope with change and choice. It can enhance or hinder personal growth and increase or decrease tendencies to self-destructiveness.

Because the sense of self, so vital to successful modern living, is rooted in early experience I would appeal particularly to the mothers of young children to try to understand these things, which are seldom, if ever, taught in baby clinics or in courses on parenthood. One way to this understanding comes from looking at the world around us and in particular at what is happening to women, and to children, and to act accordingly, with awareness of what is needed. Both boys and girls whose mothers have an awareness and understanding of these things are likely to have an easier passage and more satisfying lives than their less fortunate contemporaries. The direct impact of choice and change in society is seldom felt by young children, but their experiences in these years are crucial to their later capacity to face these things and thrive on them.

This capacity to cope with choice and change is usually first needed in adolescence and early adult life. This is when choice first becomes necessary and change apparent. The realization that their future lives will almost certainly be very different from those of their parents can come as an exciting challenge to those who are prepared for it or as a damaging shock to those who are not. Whatever their upbringing, from now on it is no longer possible to rely on parents and past supportive situations to maintain equilibrium and progress. Those who have been prepared in their childhood for choice and change find this time of life easier than those who were brought up only to follow in their parents' footsteps, particularly if this preparation was also for branching away from parents, into relationships and ways of life which parents cannot share and of which they may not approve. This is also the time when people make stable and long

term relationships and when most people choose permanent partners.

It is likely that a woman growing up today who is to succeed in the
way defined earlier will do better if she establishes herself in her own
life and in her chosen work before she embarks on marriage and
family life. This is likely to give her a stronger sense of identity, of
the way she really feels and of what she hopes to do with her life. It
will also give her more chance to see the ways in which she resembles
others and differs from them. This puts her in a better position to
make difficult choices rather than avoid them. A period of establishing herself in this way is just as valuable to the girl who feels that her
vocation in life is to be a wife and mother and that all her satisfactions
will come from this as for the girl who has other ideas or is not sure
what she wants to do. A woman who is reluctant to settle down to
family life will do better to avoid it until she feels more certain about
it, however much her parents or the community in which she lives
urge her towards it.

Once settled into parenthood many undeveloped women find it
easy to avoid choice and change by immersing themselves in husband, household and children. They do this at their peril, storing up
trouble for their later lives and for their children.

Many women with strong senses of self and developed personalities find total fulfilment in their families and they are the lucky
ones. In spite of modern technology and the diminution of essential
work in the home, it is still possible to lead a full and rewarding life as
exclusively wife and mother. But essential to this kind of success is
the awareness that it can only be temporary and there will be many
years of life left when the family is grown and gone. The successful
full-time wife and mother prepares for her future even while her
children are young.

Many young wives and mothers are not satisfied with being
nothing else. They may need to earn money or to express and
develop themselves in other ways. For these women, while their
children are young, life is full of change and choice. The ability to do
well by their families and still satisfy their personal needs depends
largely on their ability to cope with change and choice.

When a woman is middle-aged her children become independent
and disperse, and this is the time when her personal resources are put
to the test. If these are poor she is particularly liable to lapse into
self-destructivenes, often of a manipulative kind. By this time her
marriage may well have failed too, and she may be alone, or desperately trying to make new relationships. There are few more severe
tests of a woman's success or failure with herself, and anyone who
thinks about it can see it coming. Yet relatively few women who

come to this phase of life today have thought seriously about it or made plans for it. It is not surprising that this is the age at which much self-destructiveness appears for the first time, often apparently 'out of the blue'. Yet the seeds were there in the woman's earlier life, and anyone with understanding of the situation could have seen them, including the woman herself. With this understanding, she could have avoided the shock and the emptiness and made preparations for what is for many the most fulfilling and exciting time of their lives. For active life and opportunities in middle age are one of the great changes that have occurred for women in our days. These opportunities are imperfect, but they exist for every woman and the ability to make something of them, however restricted they are, is one of the hallmarks of success in women in our time. A woman's whole previous life influences her capacity to find satisfaction in the second half of her life, and to continue to live well amid an accelerating rate of change.

The same is true of old age, though this is very much influenced by the state of health and the rate of decline of physical and mental faculties. A serene and satisfying old age with plenty of interests and the capacity to communicate with younger people is a sure mark of a woman who has been successful. An old lady who can still find enjoyment and can still cope with choice is someone whom we all might hope one day to emulate.

A sense of an independent self, capacity for achievement and satisfaction, motivation, independence combined with good personal relationships, and a capacity to recognize and make choices and adapt to changes are what women need for success in the modern world. Most do better with the right man to share, though not dominate, their lives, and children in whom they foster these qualities, which will surely be needed in the future even more than they are today. Women who are unable or unwilling to strive for these things run the risk of leading dreadful lives. If they are unable to help their children to develop these qualities or, worse still, actively or covertly prevent them from doing so, then, because the changes in society are accelerating and the choices are becoming ever wider, they are preparing their children for lives even more dreadful.

Luckily most women have the capacity to develop these qualities and to help their children towards them. They and their daughters, far from contributing to our dreadful epidemic of self-destructiveness, or dreading what will happen in the future, are likely to have richer, more fulfilling and in nearly every way more satisfactory lives than their mothers and grandmothers, and their sons will make good and satisfying partners for tomorrow's women in an increasingly changing and uncertain world.

Further Reading

Alvarez, A. *The Savage God: a study of suicide* (Weidenfeld & Nicolson, London, 1971).

Arendt, Hannah. *On Revolution* (Faber & Faber, London, 1963).

Bateson, Gregory. *Steps to an Ecology of Mind* (Paladin, London, 1973).

Bowlby, John. *Separation* (Hogarth Press, London, 1973).

Brown, N.O. *Life Against Death: the psychoanalytical meaning of history* (Routledge & Kegan Paul, London, 1959).

Bullough, V.L. *The Subordinate Sex* (Penguin Books Inc, New York, 1974).

Camus, Albert. *The Myth of Sysiphus* (Alfred A. Knopf, New York, 1955).

Chafe, William H. *The American Woman* (Oxford University Press, London, 1972).

Chafe, William H. *Women & Equality* (Oxford University Press, London, 1977).

Coleridge, S.T. *Biographia Literaria*, vol.1 (Oxford University Press, London, 1907).

Dally, Ann. *Mothers: Their Power and Influence* (Weidenfeld & Nicholson, London, 1976).

Dally, Ann. *The Morbid Streak: Destructive Aspects of the Personality* (Wildwood House, London, 1978).

Durkheim, Emile. *Suicide*, trans. J.A. Spauling & G. Simpson. (Routledge & Kegan Paul, London, 1952).

Ellenberger, Henri F. *The Discovery of the Unconscious* (Allen Lane, London, 1970).

Erikson, Erik H. *Childhood and Society* (Penguin Books, Harmondsworth, 1965).

Erikson, Erik H. *Identity* (Faber & Faber, London, 1968).

Fairbairn, W.D. *Psychoanalytic Studies of the Personality* (Tavistock Publications, London, 1972).

Freud, Anna *The Ego and Mechanisms of Defence* (Hogarth Press, London, 1937).

Freud, Sigmund. *Inhibitions, Symptoms and Anxiety* (Hogarth Press, London, 1961).

Khan, M.M.R. *The Privacy of Self* (Hogarth Press, London, 1974).

Klein, Melanie. *Envy and Gratitude* (Tavistock Publications, London, 1957).

Laing, R.D. *The Divided Self* (1960) (Pelican Books, Harmondsworth, 1965).

Menninger, Karl. *Man Against Himself* (Harvest Books, copyright 1938; Harcourt Brace, London, 1972).

Mitchell, Juliet. *Psychoanalysis and Feminism* (Allen Lane, London, 1974).

Pickering, George. *Creative Malady* (Allen and Unwin, London, 1974).

Rycroft, Charles. *Anxiety and Neurosis* (Allen Lane, London, 1968).

Rycroft, Charles. *Imagination and Reality* (Hogarth Press and The Institute of Psychoanalysis, London, 1968).

Rycroft, Charles. New York Review of Books, April 3rd, 1975.

Sartre, Jean-Paul. *Being and Nothingness* (1943) (Methuen, London, 1969).

Seligman, M.E.P. *Helplessness* (Freeman, London, 1975).

Stengel, E. *Suicide and Attempted Suicide*, revised edition (Penguin Books, Harmondsworth, 1969).

Stone, Laurence. *The Family, Sex and Marriage in England 1500–1800* (Weidenfeld & Nicolson, London, 1977).

Storr, Anthony. *Human Aggression* (Allen Lane, London, 1968).

Storr, Anthony. *The Integrity of the Personality* (1960) (Pelican Books, Harmondsworth, 1963).

Tillich, Paul. *The Courage to Be* (1952) (Fontana Library, London, 1962).

Trilling, Lionel. *Sincerity and Authenticity* (Oxford University Press, London, 1972).

Winnicott, D.W. *Collected Papers* (Tavistock Publications, London, 1958).

Winnicott, D.W. *The Maturational Processes and the Facilitating Environment* (Hogarth Press, London, 1965).

Index